LIFE AFTER FAILURE

Overcoming the Hurdles to Your Success

E. Dwayne Cantrell

Life After Failure
Overcoming the Hurdles to Your Success

©2016 by E. Dwayne Cantrell

Cover photography by Ruby Z/rubizphoto.com
Cover design by Julio Norman
Book design by Jennifer Luxton/jenniferluxton.com

All Scriptures contained within are taken from the HOLY BIBLE, NEW INTERNATIONAL VERSION®. Copyright ©1973, 1978, and 1984 International Bible Society. Used with permission from Zondervan. All rights reserved.

The NIV and New International Version trademarks are registered in the United States Patent and Trademark Office by the International Bible Society. Use of either trademark requires the permission of the International Bible Society.

E. Dwayne Cantrell
dwayne@lifeafterfailure.org

*To my high school track coach whose words resound
in my life today. To my wife, children, family,
and many others who have endured all of my
failures. And to all of those who have failed and are
experiencing difficulty getting back in the race.*

TABLE OF
CONTENTS

Starting Line: *Get Up!*   08

Hurdle 1: *Revisit the Fall — Confession*   12

Hurdle 2: *Recognize the Injuries — Confrontation*   22

Hurdle 3: *Review the Race — Evaluation*   42

Hurdle 4: *Revise the Plan — Development*   58

Hurdle 5: *Run with Passion — Perseverance*   76

Finish Line: *Faith Got Up!*   96

STARTING LINE

GET UP!

I t was my junior year in high school. All year long I had prepared for this moment. My first year running hurdles in track and field and I now found myself in the city-wide qualifying meet. The race was the 300 meter hurdles. As I stood at my starting blocks, bouncing up and down with both nervous energy and excitement, my feelings unsure as to the outcome, I was determined to do all I could to win.

The official in the red coat and white hat approached the starting line with a microphone in one hand and a starter pistol in the other. As he spoke the words, "Runners take your marks," my heart rate increased as I knelt down on the track and placed my feet into the rubber-padded starting blocks. With my head bowed, I took one more deep breath as a hush fell on the entire stadium.

With silence filling the air, the official gave his final command on the microphone. "Set," he said, as he raised the starter pistol in the air. As I transitioned into running position, awaiting the sound of the gun, the length of silence seemed like an eternity. As the gun went off, I blasted out of my starting blocks with passionate determination. My focus was so intense that the only thing I could see was the hurdle in front of me, and the only sounds I could hear were my footsteps and the cadence of my breathing.

As I approached the final backstretch of the race, I noticed out of the corner of my eye the fastest runner in the stadium at my side with no other runners in sight. I was actually in position to win this race! Being that this was my first year running, I didn't realize that my goal in this preliminary race was not to win, but to simply qualify for the finals.

As we approached the final hurdle, we were running stride by stride. I could suddenly hear the roar of the crowd with cheers and applause as I was challenging the standing champion. With all of the excitement, I lost focus and hit the last hurdle. As I fell to the ground, in what felt like slow motion, I could feel my entire season and all of my hard work coming to an end. As I lay face down on the track, emotions of failure and defeat rushed over me like a waterfall. With sheer disappointment and frustration, I continued to lie there as I heard the distinct voice of my coach yell with urgency, "Get up!" Having been trained to respond to the voice of my coach, I slowly got up and, with little effort, jogged across the finish line to the sound of courteous pity applause from the audience. As soon as I crossed the finish line covered with defeat and shame, my coach vigorously approached me and said to me, "Why didn't you get right up? Do you realize how fast you were running? If you had just gotten up, you would have qualified for the finals."

The words from my high school track coach still ring in my heart today. These words have become words that I live by, and words that I impart to others. These words have guided my life's pursuits and have motivated me through failures and disappointments. "Get up!" We all find ourselves experiencing failures in life.

> **If we just learn to get up quickly, we will not only realize how close we are to the finish line, but we will be "qualified" for the next level of our journey.**

Whether we have received a failing grade on a school assignment or received low marks on a performance evaluation in the workplace, we have experienced failure. Whether we have been disciplined for mistakes made as a result of poor actions, we have experienced some type of failure. Even worse, some of us have experienced moral failure as a result of inappropriate decisions or actions, which took an emotional and spiritual toll and may have resulted in profound negative impact on those around us.

We have all experienced some form of failure, shame, disappointment, and/or personal setback. At some point in our lives, we have all found ourselves in a place where a poor decision has left us in a place of despair wondering what to do next. For some, the decision is to give up their life goals and pursuits and live lives of mediocrity out of fear of failure. For others, the decision is to give up emotionally by deciding to no longer take risks out of fear of experiencing hurt or disappointment. However, if we just learn to get up quickly, we will not only realize how close we are to the finish line, but we will be "qualified" for the next level of our journey.

As the topic of this book implies, there is life after failure. The purpose of this book is to share the steps of overcoming the various hurdles that hinder us from pursuing our destiny and experiencing victory in our lives. Though the content of this book may challenge you to revisit aspects of your past experiences, this book is not meant to be a therapeutic tool. It is simply an account of my journey and the principles I have learned from my experiences. My prayer is that through these insights you will be encouraged to get up! I pray that you would be both encouraged and inspired to walk in your God-given gifts and talents and pursue the destiny to which you have been called.

About this book

1. Each chapter of this book is composed of three sections: insights, life and discussion questions, and practical steps.

2. This book is designed to be used as an instruction book to help you through various challenges, a devotional book to encourage your spiritual walk, and a reflection book to record your thoughts and prayers.

3. You are encouraged to write in this book, share it with individuals, or use it in small and large group discussions. What is most important is that all who read this book should be encouraged and strive to experience personal and spiritual growth.

HURDLE 1

REVISIT THE FALL

"... I acknowledged my sin to you and did not cover up my iniquity. I said, 'I will confess my transgressions to the Lord.' And you forgave the guilt of my sin."

— Psalm 32:5

"Honesty is the first chapter in the book of wisdom."

— Thomas Jefferson

What happened? What went wrong? How did I fall? These are just a few questions that come to mind as I reflect on my failures in my pursuit of correction and improvement.

There are times when we simply make a bad decision or mistake. However, many times our failures are the result of a series of influences, which gradually cause us to change our beliefs and alter our practices. These alterations usually take place over time. In fact, most of the time we don't even recognize that we are changing until we have failed.

In the second quote, Thomas Jefferson reminds us, "Honesty is the first chapter in the book of wisdom." As we begin the process of living life after failure, the first hurdle that we must overcome is to address the fall. This takes both honesty and self-confrontation. The first step is to admit that something went wrong. This is not always an easy step. To admit that something went wrong in your life is to admit failure. When this happens, many of us find ourselves looking in the mirror, if you will, and seeing an image that is disturbing to us.

The story of my hurdle race serves as a foundation for me as I recall many of my failures in life. Though the majority of people who know me see me as a fairly decent individual, those who know me closely know that I have made some poor decisions and done some despicable deeds in my past.

Until recent years, much of my life has been a classic example of hypocrisy. Unfortunately, like many of the Christians portrayed in the media, I was a good person on the outside, but struggled to maintain consistent "goodness" personally. Though my heart's desire was to be the man that I strove to be, poor thinking, a wrong attitude, and bad habits resulting in negative actions caused hurt in the people closest to me and produced a lack of trust, which still remains today, from various people toward me.

Believe me — I know what it feels like to fall. Whether financially, personally, or morally, I have made poor decisions and committed wrongs that have brought shame and pain on myself, my wife and those around me. In fact, even reflecting on these things now drudges up feelings of inadequacy and shame.

I still feel shame sometimes when I recall the hurt that I have caused women throughout my life as I was pursuing my own satisfaction and battling my own personal struggles and insecurities. Though it was in the past, I still battle inadequacy at times when I think of the infidelity against my wife and the type of man that I was during that time in my life. When people trusted me, I failed them through my actions. When people believed in me, I hurt them. When women came to me for support, my distorted thoughts returned the favor with inappropriate actions. When it came to finances, my attempts to find loopholes in life led me to poor financial decisions that spiraled my household into financial ruin and enormous debt. Because of me, both my wife and I had to endure garnishments for taxes to the government and liens placed against us due to enormous credit card debt. As a father, because I was so distracted with spending many hours pursuing success, I neglected my relationships with my children. Again, on the outside I was trying to work hard to provide for my children, but deep down inside, I was trying to gain significance for myself. Even my presence at all of my kids' school events, performances and athletic contests was outwardly for them. But inwardly, my motivation was for me as I did not want to be an absent dad. The irony in all of that was though I was there physically, my mind was elsewhere and my children knew it. In my attempts to be a "good dad" my children still experienced an emotionally absent dad. I could go on, but please believe me when I say, I know what it means to fall and I know what it feels like to fail.

Natural responses to my reflections are, "Why bring up the past?" "Why dwell on this negativity?" "What's done is done." "It's over now, just move on!" Though these are common expressions to deal with our mistakes, I believe this is the easy way out. But who will teach us how to step up and own our failures? Who will walk with us as we face the crowd with our mistakes? One of the first and most important steps on our road to success is to acknowledge and confess the failure.

Confess the failure

What happened? Though honesty is important in all areas of our lives, it is in this stage that honesty is vital if we want to experience change. Like the individual who meets with the priest in the confessional booth or the person in the interrogation room after the commission of a crime, confession is an honest statement of what actually happened.

Depending on the level of failure (as we perceive it) this step may not be as easy as it sounds. It can be difficult to say the words, "I failed," "I messed up," "I made a mistake," or "I was wrong." Though statements like these are a good start, the type of confession needed for true change must be more specific, and may be more difficult to carry out. For true change, one must have the courage to make statements like:

"I failed when I _____."

"I messed up by doing _____."

"I made the mistake of _____."

"I was wrong when I _____."

However, when discussing failure, one of the hindrances to our honesty is blaming. Like the story of Adam and Eve in the Garden of Eden when he was confronted about the wrong that was committed, his first response was to blame God. Does this tendency exist with us today? What excuses do we use when we are confronted with a wrong that we have committed? Who do we blame when something goes wrong in our lives?

Another hindrance to our confession is denial. I have heard many people say that there is no such thing as failure. I have heard people say that they have never failed in life — that they have only had experiences that led them down an unexpected path.

While the finality and the nuances of failing can be debated, the concept of failing is real. Though one may disagree with this system of evaluation, a student who receives an F on a report card has been informed by the instructor that he/she has failed to perform in a satisfactory manner. An employee who receives the lowest score possible on a performance evaluation has been informed by the employer that he/she has failed to perform in a satisfactory manner. A low credit score is an indicator that an individual has failed to maintain timely payments on their debts.

While it is true that mistakes and poor decisions may result in failure, it is also true that wrong behavior is a significant contributor to failure. Philosophers of ethics may disagree with a black-and-white concept of right and wrong. However, those who subscribe to biblical principles as their foundation for living know that wrong is real. For the Christian, anything that is contrary to biblical teachings is considered sin.

One of my personal frustrations is how loosely we use the word sin, which has resulted in a variety of interpretations. Therefore, for the purpose of this lesson, I have defined sin as Satisfying Your Inner Nature (SIN). All of us are born with an inner nature that desires to be satisfied. As babies, we cried when we needed milk or our diaper changed. As we became toddlers, we learned that crying was the mechanism for requesting, and many times obtaining, the things we desired. When we wanted toys, or a particular treat, we cried when we didn't receive them.

In and of itself, there is nothing inherently wrong with desiring things. However, there is another side of us that cries out for the wrong reasons. Reflecting back to infancy, most children emphatically used the word, "Mine," to indicate their rights to their possessions. This eventually results in the lack of desire to share what they have. In short, all of us have within us an innate selfishness.

As we grow older, especially in this day and age, many of us have a desire to overindulge in material possessions, and when we get them we only go so far in sharing them (if we share them at all). When purchasing that brand-new car and driving it off the

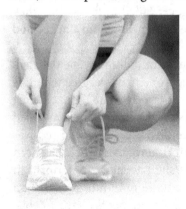

lot, for many, the word, "Mine," would come to mind if someone who is not particularly close asked to take it for a spin.

Going deeper, as we grow older, our inner "Mine" can tempt us to crave one thing that we believe we deserve, but that one thing can lead to our demise. Though it seems so simple, it carries with it a weight of selfishness that is, many times, not even recognized. That one thing we desire, that one area of selfishness or itch that when scratched would lead us down a road of failure, is one of sheer irony. That one thing is called happiness. At its core, happiness is something we experience that causes pleasure. In our pursuit of happiness, our inner nature's desire is to experience pleasure.

At the onset, this may seem harmless. However this pursuit of self-satisfaction can, and does, lead to destruction. I recall going to Las Vegas for a business trip and noticing one thing. It seemed that no matter what you desire, you can overindulge in it in Las Vegas. Whether you desire the exciting rush that comes from gambling, the high that comes from dancing and well-mixed drinks, the readily available opportunities for sexual engagement (even prostitution is legal in Las Vegas), or the seemingly harmless array of delectable buffet dining, almost every option and opportunity is available to Satisfy Your Inner Nature. It should be no surprise, then, that Las Vegas is referred to as Sin City.

> **As we grow older our inner "Mine" can tempt us to crave one thing that we believe we deserve, but that one thing can lead to our demise.**

These indulgences are not just satisfied on vacation, but these are daily temptations. In our community, we find those who spend many hours in their jobs and very little, if any, time with their children in their effort to satisfy their desire for self-importance and success. We find people who are not happy with their spouses so they find comfort in pornography or company with another companion to satisfy their desire to be desired. There are others who find difficulty coping with the challenges of life so they turn to drugs, alcohol, or even food to escape from pain.

Though there are many other examples, the common denominator to these actions is the negative consequences that follow. Minimally, the consequences we receive as the result of our actions is the loss of time, which, to many, is very important. However, the greatest consequence is the loss of trust from loved ones, the dissolution of marriages, the continued cycle of negative behavior transferred to our children, and, in some cases, death it-self. There are many reasons for our indulgences, however the desire and result is still to Satisfy Our Inner Nature. So what are we to do to avoid SIN and the consequences thereof? When we fall into this category, confession can be a bit more challenging. However it is critical that we do so if we want to move toward our purpose. James 5:16 tells us to, "Confess your sins to each other and pray for each other so that you may be healed." According to this text, healing is derived from confession and prayer.

The first thing to note, which should serve as a lifetime re-minder, is that we can't do this on our own. Having someone in whom we can confide and a place where we can make safe con-fessions is important. Some use a priest in the confines of a con-fessional. Some utilize the services of a counselor or a therapist in the confines of an office. Yet others make use of a trusted and wise friend on a park bench or at a kitchen table. Whatever the case, we need people of integrity in our lives to share our confes-sions with.

Then we need prayer. We need to pray for our own strength and the courage to confess our sins. We need to pray for God to lead us to insightful confidants who will not judge us, but will of-fer us both comfort and loving correction. Finally, we need those who will partner in prayer with us as we look in the mirror and see reflection of our faults with honest eyes, broken hearts, and sober minds.

The good news is that if we confess our sins to one another and pray for each other then we can be healed. Whether we have failed because of SIN or as a result of poor decisions, confession and prayer can bring the healing needed to overcome the first hurdle to our destiny.

LIFE QUESTIONS

1. What is your belief about the concept of failure?

2. What does happiness mean to you? Do you believe that we should pursue happiness in life?

3. Is there an area in you life where you believe that you have failed (or continue to fail in) that is hindering you from reaching your potential in life?

4. Do you find difficulty in confessing your failures? Why or why not?

5. Do you have people to whom you can confess your sins? If no, why not? If so, what qualifies them?

PRACTICAL STEPS

Step 1: Take inventory of your life.

As difficult as this may be, the first step is to take an honest inventory of your life and identify areas where you have failed, fallen short, or missed the mark (or whatever terminology you would like to use). Though it is difficult to dig up past dirt, or even focus on our flaws, this step is important if we want to overcome this hurdle.

Step 2: Confess.

After finding our areas of failure, the next step is to confess them specifically. We need to first make this confession to ourselves. Then we need to make this confession to God. Not because our Creator does not already know everything about us, but because doing so brings us into honest spiritual relationship and intimacy with Him.

Step 3: Find a confidant.

If we don't have someone already, we need to seek out a person, or persons, in whom we can confide. This is the step where we confess to another person or persons. This can be an individual or a small group. This must be more than a poker buddy or a group of girls. The character of people who will receive your confessions must consist of the following:

- **Integrity:** This is a person who will be honest, keep God first, and help you to keep God first in all that you do.

- **Wisdom:** This is a person who knows when to keep confidence and when to help you to seek further attention.

- **Compassion:** This is a person who will not punish you with your confession, but will listen with love and offer you loving insight and correction when needed.

PERSONAL PRAYERS/REFLECTIONS

RECOGNIZE THE INJURIES

"You were running a good race. Who cut in on you and kept you from obeying the truth? That kind of persuasion does not come from the one who calls you."

—Galatians 5:7-8

"I don't measure a man's success by how high he climbs, but how high he bounces when he hits the bottom."

—General George Patton

I had the opportunity to run track in college. I was nowhere close to being a star athlete, but there were many meaningful lessons learned from the experience. At the college level, it was both fun and challenging. At times it felt like the coach received personal pleasure from seeing us suffer through grueling workouts. I can recall the first few weeks of practice in my freshman year. Many of the athletes were suddenly missing from practice. Word came back to the coach that his runners were spending time in the training room, seeking attention for their pain (or skipping out on practice).

When the coach learned about this, he ensured that all of his athletes were at the next practice. Before practice began, he gave a speech and taught us a lesson that, to this day, I have never forgotten. "There is something that I need everyone to understand," he said. "There is a difference between pain and injury. You are supposed to be in pain. Pain is part of the process. You learn to work through pain. If I find out that anyone of you is in the training room because of pain then you'll have to answer to me. Now injury is different. If you are truly injured then get to the training room so you can get treatment."

These words have remained with me well into my adulthood. Whether coaching high school sports, working with teens and troubled youth, or providing pastoral counseling for men and married couples, these words have held true in physical, emotional, and spiritual form. There is, indeed, a difference between pain and injury.

The first quote above is an excerpt from the apostle Paul's letter to the church in Galatia. He is addressing a group of people who adopted the Christian faith and, in the beginning, were walking in freedom. However, at some point on their Christian journey, they encountered people who began to have a negative influence on them, persuading them to adapt beliefs and practices that were contrary to their faith, which resulted in undue strain and conflict in their walk.

Like this group of people, there are times in our lives when we start off doing well in a given area, however over time, the negative influences persuade us to adapt beliefs and practices, which are contrary to the truth. It is terrible what women must endure in our society when it comes to the idea of beauty. Though I am a man, I am a father of a daughter who was teased about her hair and nonverbally challenged about the shade of her skin color when she was younger. Seeing images of girls and women in magazines and on television who are coined as "beautiful" eventually persuaded my then-thirteen-year-old, size-three daughter to utter the words, "I'm fat ... I need to lose weight." When my daughter was a toddler, she didn't have these concerns. Who cut in on her? Allow me to go a little deeper. I can't tell you exactly what age this happened to me, but as a child I distinctly recall walking into the apartment of a close relative and finding a magazine on the coffee table. This magazine had a picture of a beautiful woman on the cover, and as I turned the pages, I was confronted with multiple beautiful women in provocative positions, wearing little to no clothing. This turned a switch on inside of me that would change my life. As I went into school, I remember a kid bringing another magazine of this type and sharing it with a group of us. When I was at home, I found a few of these magazines hidden in different places. At another friend's house, this was taken to

It is important to know the difference between pain and injury in our lives.

a different level. My friend's parents had a stash of videos, which my friend had found. As we were hanging out at his house, he placed a movie into the video player, and I was introduced to my first pornographic movie. All of this happened before I reached high school. As a pre-adolescent I was exposed to pornography and, listening to relatives engaged in sexual activity with their partners. This had a profound impact on me. The irony is that when I talked about this with other friends or relatives, the response was as though this was just were a normal part of life. However, what was supposed to be normal caused a hypersexuality in me that felt anything but normal. As a child, who cut in on me? Is this what children are supposed to experience in life? Was my life interrupted by corruption? Was my innocence taken from me at a young age? The answer is Yes. There are times when we experience hurts and disappointments in

life. I associate these with pain. And borrowing the words of my college track coach, we need to push through pain. However, there are experiences that leave lasting effects on us. If these are unresolved they can have negative implications on us and on others around us. These are what I refer to as injuries. And I agree that injuries need to be treated.

It is important to know the difference between pain and injury in our lives. This is a good time to consider the popular phrase, "Get over it!" Some people in our lives will suggest that if there is something in our way we just need to get over it. If we have any fears, doubts, insecurities, rejection, or hurts, then we just need to shake them off and get on with our lives. They will suggest that if we experience pain, then we need to grow up, put on our big-boy or big-girl pants, and move on. These sentiments almost imply that a sign of maturity is to take the experiences of life and just move on without addressing them. Just shake it off and get over it! The challenge in this approach is that if you just "shake it off" without analyzing how you got there in the first place, you will find yourself in an endless cycle of being in the dumps and shaking it off all of the time. This type of cycle can be both exhausting and defeating. Just like an injury, if left untreated, these life issues can cause long-term damage in ourselves and to others around us.

What I have learned over the years is that if I want to move on from my past and become the man that God has created, designed, purposed, and equipped me to be, then I must go back and confront my past. Without confronting my past, I will continue to carry bad habits, poor thinking, selfish ideologies, and negative behavior into my future. I have realized that carrying these behaviors into my future will not stop with me (since they did not start with me), but they will be passed down to my chil-

25

dren and generations after them. With that said, since we all have had negative experiences in our lives, I will discuss how to process the pain, and how to analyze the injuries.

Process the pain

In discussing the difference between pain and injury, let's first discuss the process of pain. When we fail, there is usually a reason for it, which we will discuss later. However, there is also some type of pain associated with failure. Many times, failure happens when we have listened to the wrong voice in our head, gone the wrong direction and now suffered the consequences from that decision.

Like a pebble in one's shoe, for many of us it is irritating to know that there is an area of temptation in our lives that we can do nothing about. For some, that area is anger where you allow people to send you to a high level of anger with minimal effort on their part. For others, that area is emotion where, like anger, one minor event or statement from another can trigger an array of emotions that you allow to affect your whole day. Others are tempted by visual stimulation where viewing images of, or having actual interaction with, the opposite sex, can put you in a position where you allow yourself to travel down a road of regret.

Not only do we have the torment of always having to be on guard to make the right decisions, we must endure the pain that results from the consequences of making wrong decisions. We will focus on the actual consequences in a later chapter, but for a moment, let's turn our attention to the pain associated with failure. In my history of visits with doctors, whether as an athlete or a general patient, eventually I would always hear the same question, "Where does it hurt?" If you call into a medical help line you will usually speak to a medical professional that will ask you to describe what you are feeling. This is how they diagnose your symptoms to arrive at a recommendation for treatment.

The same is true in overcoming this hurdle in our lives after failure. We have to assess the pain by asking ourselves, "Where does it hurt?" We have to give a self-diagnosis by challenging ourselves to describe what we are feeling. Again, whether we fail due to poor decisions, or due to acts of SIN (**S**atisfying **O**ur **I**nner Nature) against God, we can experience a variety of feelings.

You will notice how I created an acrostic with the word SIN and used my personal descriptor of Satisfying Your Inner Nature. It is my inner nature that desires, craves, and needs. It is not a sin to have certain desires. We long for love, we long for understanding, we long for justice, and we desire pleasure and enjoyment. However, there are times when our inner nature can be insatiable or reaches a state of dysfunction. When we do not receive love in a functional manner, we can resort to dysfunctional methods to achieve it. We can connect to the wrong people or end up compromising our morals for moments of connection. When we do not receive justice or fairness, we can resort to taking matters in our own hands and causing harm to others through our words or deeds. And sometimes when we experience painful situations in lives, our inner nature can have a tendency to gravitate toward methods or substances to give us temporary relief. When we do this, not only do we fail to address the real problem, but we can end up regretting the decisions we have made in Satisfying Our Inner Nature. This is when we can move from simply making poor decisions to conscious decisions that satisfy ourselves rather than God. This can result in moral failure.

One might ask, "How do I get through this type of shame?" The good news is that it can be done.

Having personally experienced moral failure, the primary feeling that covered me like a heavy blanket was shame. I was embarrassed to literally look at myself in a mirror because of the ugliness I perceived in the person at which I was looking. I was embarrassed to look my wife in the face because of my failure as a husband. My confidence with my children was gone because of my failure as a father. My relationships with certain friends and family members were altered, and I walked around daily wondering if someone else had learned about my failure and how they were going to treat me. I felt sick to my stomach at work, and walking through the doors of the church felt like I was walking down the corridors to the throne of God only to see the disappointing look on my Heavenly Father's face as He saw this horrible son darkening His presence.

Though this may sound like an exaggeration, these were my actual feelings and perceptions. This was real for me, and I know that others can identify with these feelings. One might ask, "How do I get through this type of shame?" The good news is that it can be done. The challenging news is that, in my experience, very few can manage the next level of pain that it takes.

There are few that have the strength or the patience that it takes to stand on God. God's response to Paul in 2 Corinthians 12:9: "… my grace is sufficient … for my power is made perfect in weakness." Returning to the words of General Patton, "I don't measure a man's success by how high he climbs, but how high he bounces when he hits the bottom," the question becomes, "Who can sustain the impact of hitting the bottom?"

If the first level of pain is weakness in the area of temptation that we continue to struggle with, which we cannot seem to eliminate, and the second level of pain is the array of negative feelings associated with failure, then the third level of pain is the fight against all of the emotional trauma and negative feelings that we must endure in order to overcome this hurdle. In other words, if we want to experience God's perfect power, we must endure our perfect weakness.

In order to bounce back from failure, we must endure the impact of the fall. If you have ever bounced a ball on the ground, you have noticed that the harder you bounce it on the ground, the higher it will go into the air. This illustration holds true with us. The harder we fall, the higher we will rise when we bounce back … if we endure the impact. So how do we endure the impact of failure? How do we endure the emotional pain? How do we endure the psychological blows? We must fight!

What do I mean by fight? This is a fight for freedom. One thing that we are taught in the Christian church is that salvation is free. This is the gospel and it is, indeed, good news. The fact that Jesus lived a life of total sacrifice and complete surrender — even of life itself as he died on a cross for our sins that we might have eternal life by believing in him — is good news.

The irony, however, is that though salvation is free, and eternal life is free, freedom itself is not free. Freedom comes with a price. Whether we're talking about America's freedom from British rule or the civil rights movement, the fight for freedom is a hard-fought battle with bloodshed and multiple casualties. When we talk about freedom from addictions, there is a hard-fought battle both mentally and physically to overcome the grip that has taken hold of the individual. Even for those who under false philosophies and ideologies of defeat and failure that have them living below their potential, there is a fight required to overcome these false beliefs. But make no mistake, in the fight for freedom, there will be pain and there will be casualties. Something must, and will, die at the end of this fight.

> **Though it is true that the Lord will fight our battles, we have to fight against temptations, we have to ward off thoughts of negativity and defeat, and we have to fight daily against our worst adversary ... ourselves.**

As Frederick Douglass so eloquently stated in his famous freedom speech, "This struggle may be moral, or it may be physical, or it may be both moral and physical, but it must be a struggle." The fight for our physical, emotional, or spiritual freedom comes with a price. As Christians, we can't just sit back and wait for God to pick us up and carry us to victory. Though it is true that the Lord will fight our battles, we have to fight against temptations, we have to ward off thoughts of negativity and defeat, and we have to fight daily against our worst adversary ... ourselves.

As a result of our fight, as previously mentioned, something must die. Our old habits must die. Our old thought processes must die. Our beliefs in the many lies of who we are not and what we cannot do must die. Our contentment with mediocrity must die. Our understanding that failure is finality must die. The quit in us must die!

The problem is that most people I have come across are either not willing to fight this battle for freedom or are tired of fighting altogether. In his book *No More Excuses*, renowned pastor, author, and professor, Dr. Tony Evans, states it this way, "Having become frustrated by the inability of their increased efforts to produce the joy, peace, power, and victory they have heard so much about, many believers have simply given up the struggle and have allowed themselves to sink in the quicksand of spiritual defeat, accepting it as their lot in life."

Has this ever been true for you? Have you ever been at the point where you were just tired of fighting? Have you ever just become worn out to the point where you raised the white flag of surrender just to experience some temporary peace in your life? Have you ever found yourself in a place where you would rather live in the peace of defeat than have to sustain the battle wounds required for victory?

For many of us, we are not ready to either engage in, or re-engage in the fight for change until we have reached the breaking point in our hearts, and arrive at the popular phrase, "Enough is enough!" Once we have reached our breaking points, and desire change in our lives, we must engage in fighting our way out of this gripping enslavement of shame, self-anger, self-disappointment, and the many other feelings associated with failure.

However, if we want to change, these things must die. For when these things die and we let go of our own processes, we make ourselves vulnerable, even weak, before God, allowing Him to display His strength through us. This is how He is strong in our weaknesses. Though the process of honesty, confession of our weaknesses, presentation of ourselves naked before God, and the unveiling of all of our frailties, blemishes and poor qualities is a painful and shameful process, this is a crucial aspect of recovery and freedom in Christ.

From the beginning, we see the pain of shame and the painful process of restoration. According to Genesis 3, Adam and Eve sinned against God in the Garden of Eden. Feeling the painful shame of disobeying God, they hid from him and covered themselves with fig leaves to hide their nakedness. God told them to come out from hiding. After he administered consequences to them for their sins, they went on to fulfill their commission from God to "be fruitful and increase in number; fill the earth and subdue it."

Thus, from this example we see a model for dealing with the pain of failure.

Come out of hiding

If we honestly want to deal with the pain in our lives, the first thing we must do is come out from our hiding place. Many children have special hiding places that they establish when they are playing. Children also have special hiding places to which they retreat when they are afraid. Places like the closet or under the bed are most common for children to take refuge to seek protection from the scary things in their lives.

As adults, we also have special hiding places that we run to when we are afraid. However, the places to which we run are less conspicuous. As adults, we tend to seek refuge at work, in friends, with volunteer organizations, in extracurricular activities, and even in our children. These areas in and of themselves are not bad, but when we use them to hide from our pain, we will never improve. Many of us, however, have more destructive hiding places. Alcohol, drugs, pornography, inappropriate relationships, and many others become hiding place in an effort to seek refuge from pain. Though these hiding places may ease the pain momentarily, when the high of these destructive activities wears off, the pain is only heightened.

In dealing with pain, we must come out of our hiding places and stand before God. Though it is embarrassing to bring forth the things that we have hidden in our "closets" and under our "beds," it is very difficult to let go of these things that have faithfully provided us comfort throughout our lives, and we must rid ourselves of these hiding places if we ever want to live in true freedom.

Face your consequences

The second difficult, but essential, component derived from our sample text is that of being man or woman enough to face our consequences. Every action has a reaction. Every positive thing that we do yields benefits, and every negative thing that we do yields consequences. This is true whether we are aware of it or not.

The reality is that whether we fail at a task, fail in our purpose by becoming distracted, or fail morally, there are consequences to failure. These consequences may be as minimal as wasted time, or as monumental as prison time. Whatever the consequences God is calling us to come out and face them.

The irony of our hiding places is that they encourage our belief that hiding from our consequences keeps us safe, when in fact hiding only delays the consequences, takes precious time away from our lives, and hinders us from reaching our potential in Christ. The truth is though there are consequences from failing, if we actually face them the consequences turn into learning experiences. What we think are negative implications of failure are actually necessary catalysts that can be used to propel us toward success. If we could just have the courage to know that if we stand before God, even with our shame, God will walk with us and help us to endure all of the elements necessary to break us of our former selves, and help us to become the people that he created us to be.

Continue in your purpose

In the Adam and Eve illustration, the text states that their original purpose before they sinned was to be fruitful and increase and subdue this earth. In other words, God created them to be people of increase and authority. Notice that the emphasis of their increase was what they left in the earth, not what they took out of the earth. Their purpose was to be productive, filling this earth with people and taking charge of the things on it. The purpose given to Adam and Eve has not changed with us. Our marching orders as men and women on this planet are still in effect. We are to be people who increase and enhance this earth and take authority of the things in it.

This has little to do with how many things we accumulate and how many of the earth's resources we consume for our personal pleasures. This has everything to do with being productive about increasing ourselves to be our best selves so that we can be productive in encouraging the next generation to be their best selves.

Furthermore, our purpose is to be people who take authority over the things in this world, including ourselves. Self and selfishness must die if we want to live lives of purpose. Our free selves must be freely poured out throughout this world to promote the generational furtherance of a people who can experience true freedom in Christ.

Just as Christ died so that we might have life, we too must die in ourselves so that others might live. Thus our purpose is people. And in order for us to fulfill our purpose, we must be free.

There is one more very important aspect of the Adam and Eve story. Their purpose before they failed did not change afterward. They were people of promise and authority before the fall, and they continued to be people of promise and authority after they got back up. God did not relegate them to their consequences; He repositioned them in their purpose. This is also true for us. When we fail, it is important to understand that we are not failures. We are not failures who have purpose hidden within us — we are people of purpose who fell. When we get back up, we remain people of purpose. The difference is, with the right perspective, we will rise wiser and stronger than before we fell.

Analyze the injuries

At the beginning of this chapter, I shared the words of my college track coach, "There is a difference between pain and injury ... Pain is part of the process. You learn to work through pain ... Now injury is different. If you are truly injured then get to the training room so you can get treatment."

We have discussed the process of pain and the fight required to overcome it. We have discussed the idea of facing and working through pain. However, injury is very different. As an athlete, when you are truly injured, playing through injury can make the injury worse. You may have seen professional athletes who have chosen to continue to compete throughout their careers with long-lasting injuries only to find themselves with permanent ailments when they retire.

You have, no doubt, seen the boxer who sustained multiple injuries to the head during his career suffering permanent brain damage throughout the rest of his life. You may have heard of the many collegiate and professional football players who, long after retirement, find difficulty sleeping at night due to permanent joint pains brought on by years of physical impact. You may have even heard of former collegiate and professional basketball players who suffer from permanent back and knee pains.

There is a difference between pain and injury, and knowing the difference can have lifelong implications. Pain is easily identified because you actually feel where it hurts. However, an injury takes more probing to identify. For example, people can have pain in their knees that is a result of having undetected problems with their feet (this is just an analogy, but I hope you can see the point). The pain in the knees is a symptom, but the problem is with the feet. You can continue to treat the symptom, but real healing will not come until the real problem is treated.

There is a difference between pain and injury, and knowing the difference can have lifelong implications.

This is also true with our lives. When we are emotionally or psychologically injured, many symptoms are displayed. I have personal experience with what I refer to as psychological injury. Having been exposed to pornographic material and experiencing sexual activity as a child, my view of women and purity were destroyed at an early age. Having examples of men in my life who were unfaithful, promiscuous, and who treated women like objects gave me the mentality and desire to do the same.

As a youth, having certain friends who shared the same thoughts, engaged in the viewing of pornographic material, and participated in sexual activity affirmed my beliefs and behavior. All of these things lead me into a life of sexual misconduct and addictive behavior. The interesting fact is that most of my activity was perceived to be normal conduct for a man in our society. Most of my actions could be categorized in alpha male or, the "That's just how guys are" category. Experiences as a college athlete and living in a fraternity house further exacerbated my sexual activity and objectification of women. Again, most of my activity seemed normal for a guy and in fact, seemed to attract more women to me. However, these behaviors led to many broken relationships, and many women whose hearts I damaged, including that of my own wife.

It wasn't until I accepted Christ into my life that these behaviors came into conflict with my newly adapted belief system. As I came to Christ and embraced biblical teachings, I developed a desire to want to be a new man. I wanted to be a man that God would be proud of. I wanted to be a man who was faithful and who could be trusted. I wanted to be a man who no longer had the desire to be unfaithful, or to have inappropriate video tapes and magazines hidden throughout my house.

Though I had such noble desires, achieving this level of faithfulness would prove to be a struggle as this would be in conflict with everything that I had known for the majority of my life. How would I break through to becoming a new man? How would I stop the contradiction between my beliefs, my behaviors, and living my life as a classic Christian hypocrite? This challenge would require personal reflection and confrontation. The questions would be, "Were these pains that could be worked through one by one?" "Had I sustained an injury somewhere in my past that needed to be corrected?" Did I need to simply read my Bible more, pray more, and stop doing those specific acts to become the man that God called me to be?

The fact is that I tried as hard as I could to immerse myself in the Bible and pray with tears in my eyes for God to change me. This only heightened my spiritual awareness of how wrong I was and the conflict grew stronger. Like the apostle Paul in Romans 7:14 wrote, "I do not understand what I do. For what I want to do I do not do, but what I hate I do." This was my Christian conflict. When I did the wrong thing and made the wrong decisions, deep inside, this was not the way that I wanted to live. So what was I to do if I wanted to change?

This is where the illustrations of pain and injury comes in. Remember, according to our illustration, pain is something that can be worked through. Thus, changing my actions was something that I had to do in order to live as a man of integrity. However, simply changing my behavior would not address the real problem. The fact is that every action that I did was a symptom of a deeper problem. The fact is that an injury took place early in my life.

Again, when a physical injury takes place, in order to make a proper diagnosis and receive the proper treatment, one must seek the assistance of a physician. I believe that the same is true emotionally and psychologically. If I was going to be successful in treating the real problem, I would need to seek the assistance of a Christian counselor. One might ask, "Why a Christian counselor?" I believe that if one wants to be a better mechanic, the one should consult the insight of a more experienced mechanic. Likewise, I believe that if one wants to deal with the root of psycho-emotional behaviors as a Christian, then one should consult a Christian who is trained in dealing with such issues.

Hence, my participation in Christian counseling with a trained therapist began. It is important to know that the first thing the therapist said to me was, "With all of the trauma that you faced as a child, it is a wonder that you can still function. God has definitely covered you." What I learned through counseling is that the injury that I sustained as a child was to my thought process. All of my attitudes and actions centered on my desire to be affirmed as a man. My desire was to be valued, loved, and important. Through all of my actions, my desire was to have significance and to be loved by others.

The task at hand for me was one that Paul commands in Romans 12, "Do not conform any longer to the pattern of this world, but be transformed by the renewing of your mind. Then you will be able to test and approve what God's will is — his good, pleasing, and perfect will." In order to become a man of God, I needed to have a transformation of my mind so that I could recognize and do the things that are pleasing to God.

Therefore, the first action that the counselor took was to pray over me, and the first assignment that he gave me was to memorize a Bible verse (which I still stand by today). The difference between what he did and what I was able to do on my own is that I had a person with insight who could give me specific tools and strategies and hold me accountable as I progressed through this process.

I had to be honest, transparent, and serious about confronting this problem and dealing with this injury. I had to come to a place in my life where I was broken enough to realize that the damage that I was causing to others needed to change. However, I also had to realize that God created me and called me to do great things on this earth. If I were going to accomplish any of those great things in life, I was going to have to change. Make no mistake though — I needed the help of another to get through this process — this awareness only came through revelation from the Holy Spirit as I committed myself to Scripture and prayer.

To this day, I still experience inner conflict of doing right and wrong, but I am able to make better choices and pursue the things of life to which God has called me because of the insight and strength that he gave me to confront my injuries.

Let me pause here for a moment and address the fact of choice. Though my environment and my circumstances taught and shaped me, there came a point in my life where these became my choices. You might say that I was a victim as a child, but my becoming a victimizer was my choice. This may sound like I am being harsh on myself, but I can't blame my actions on anyone but myself. Though I get angry that the environment in which I grew up was not my choice, and the things to which I was pre-disposed were not my choice, I take ownership and responsibility for my actions. Because in the end, it was my choice to get help so that I could take the proper steps to becoming a better man for my God, my wife and my children.

So what do you choose? Do you choose to examine your injuries or do you want to spend your life simply playing through the pain? Are you tired of thinking about your past and fighting the fight of pressing through the pain? Have you given up the fight? Like avoiding medical and dental checkups, ignoring psycho-emotional injuries can lead to permanent damage. This damage will not only affect you, but the people around you and generations after you. You may have seen track races on television where a runner falls and causes others to trip over him, resulting in injury to others. In the same way, your fall can cause you to be a stumbling block for others, thus negatively impacting their lives as well as yours. The good news is that there is help available to get you back on track if you are bold enough to examine your injuries and seek the help needed to heal them.

LIFE QUESTIONS

1. What areas of your life have you given up due to fear of failure?

2. Why is self-confrontation important if you want to move forward in life?

3. In your opinion, what are the differences between pain and injury in life?

4. In what ways are your past experiences negatively impacting your present outlook on/pursuits in life?

5. What does it take for people to seek professional help?

PRACTICAL STEPS

Step 1: Change your view of pain and sacrifice.

Many people do not like to deal with emotional pain. However, pain is necessary for improvement. If you have ever begun an exercise program to improve your physical health you have experienced the pain involved as your body endures physical changes. If you have ever begun an academic training program for a certification or a degree you have noticed the amount of sacrifice and intellectual stretching that occurs through the process. If this is required of most other improvement activities in life, why would we think this is not needed emotionally? Pain, sacrifice, and endurance are necessary if we want to improve. Understanding this will add purpose to our fight.

Step 2: Change your direction.

When you have come to the place where you are tired of living in defeat, follow the instructions as expressed in 2 Chronicles 7:14: "If my people, who are called by my name, will humble themselves and pray and seek my face and turn from their wicked ways, then will I hear from heaven and will forgive their sin and will heal their land."

- As Christians, we must humble ourselves and realize that we cannot make it on our own … we must seek God.

- We must turn from our wicked ways. Turning from our wicked ways and walking in the right direction is called repentance. If we want God to heal our land, our hearts, and our lives, we must turn away from our wicked ways to Him.

Step 3: Practice forgiveness.

As we review our failings and fight the fight of pursuing our purpose, we will experience a host of feelings. In order for us to move from the past to the future, forgiveness is an important step. We must forgive those who have hurt, disappointed, abandoned and even violated us. Doing this will release us from the shackles of dysfunctional emotional connections to those with whom we are angry. This will also clear our lenses to recognize that those people have hurts of their own and are in need of God's help. We must also forgive ourselves. The Bible tells us that, "If we confess our sins, [God] is faithful and just and will forgive us our sins and purify us from all unrighteousness." If God Almighty has forgiven us, who are we to usurp His power by refusing to forgive ourselves? We must realize that, in order to walk in freedom, forgiveness of both self and others is vital.

Step 4: Recognize when you are treating the symptoms versus treating the problem.

If you have ever taken a CPR or first aid class you would know that when a person either stops breathing or is injured there are immediate steps that need to be taken to sustain the individual. By either helping someone to breathe or providing bandages for wounds, you may help sustain a person. However, these treatments are only temporary. The individual must be taken to the hospital for further evaluation and treatment. This is the same with us emotionally. There are times when making immediate adjustments and changes will fix our problems. However, as mentioned in the previous chapter, when we experience injury, we need to seek help from a professional (e.g., clergy or Christian counselor) for regular evaluation and treatment.

PERSONAL PRAYERS/REFLECTIONS

REVIEW THE RACE

"Search me, O God, and know my heart; test me and know my anxious thoughts. See if there is any offensive way in me, and lead me in the way everlasting."

— Psalm 139:23-24

"Insanity: doing the same thing over and over again and expecting different results."

— Albert Einstein

As both an athlete and coach, one tool that was used for preparation was video. In football, video was taken of practices and games. At a designated time, the team would come together in small groups (usually by position) and review the video. The purpose of this review was twofold. First, it was important to watch ourselves individually to see what we did correctly and where we made mistakes. A coach could tell us these things, but when we saw these things for ourselves, a different impact was made.

Second, reviewing video was a way of recognizing effective and ineffective tendencies in both ourselves and our opponents. In sports where participants oppose one another, such as team sports (football, baseball, basketball, soccer, etc.) and individual sports (tennis, boxing, fencing, etc.), video is a key tool in determining which weaknesses of the opponent could be exploited in order to achieve victory.

However, if you participate in a sport like track and field, there is no opposition. Though you are competing against others, there is no offense or defense. You are actually competing against yourself. Your only goal is to jump higher, throw farther, leap longer, or run faster than everyone else. With few exceptions (distance races for example), spending time analyzing the tendencies of others is useless.

This is especially true with running hurdles. With hurdles, your objective is to leap over the hurdles and get to the finish line faster than your opponents. To do this, all of your strategy is focused on you and the hurdle. In other words, the hurdle is your only true opponent. In order to effectively and efficiently navigate these hurdles, speed and technique are paramount.

This is where the use of video comes into play in this sport. As my coaches did with me, and as I did with the athletes that I coached, video footage was taken from various angles during practice. As I reviewed the footage, I was looking for tendencies, both good and bad, in order to maximize effectiveness. In short, the goal of video was to get the athlete to do more of the good things, and less of the bad things to become a more competitive athlete. The ultimate goal was to get to the finish line as quickly and efficiently as possible. Likewise, as we navigate our Christian journey and pursue our purpose, our desire should be to get there as quickly and efficiently as possible.

I can still remember my first hurdle race like it was yesterday. As I approached the starting line and stood in my lane, I looked from left to right in front of me and there were eight lanes on the track, each with a hurdles in them forming what appeared to be a fairly tall wall across track, and a series of walls from start to finish. It literally looked like walls of hurdles as far as the eye could see. Standing at the starting line, there seemed to be no end in sight. And because my lane was toward the middle of the track, I could see that once I started this race, there was no turning back. I could not go around these "walls" because there were people on either side of me. Though these hurdles were pretty tall, they were too short to run under them. And I was too new at running hurdles to know that if I got into trouble I could simply stop running. Nonetheless, one truth was clear: the only way to get to the finish line was to get over every hurdle.

The only way to finish the race of life successfully is to get over every hurdle.

As Christians, we must embrace this same truth. As we run this race of life, we all have hurdles in our lanes; the only way to finish this race of life successfully is to get over every hurdle. We must continually improve our practices of faith if we want to be stronger in our walk with Christ. We cannot improve if we remain stagnant in our practices. Because none of us are perfect, we all have negative tendencies and bad habits that need to be constantly reviewed. Without this review, and making changes where necessary, there is no way that we will ever improve. In the words of Albert Einstein, insanity is, "… doing the same thing over and over again and expecting different results." Therefore, we need to regularly take the time to review the positive tendencies and bad habits in our lives so that we can learn to do more of the good things and less of the bad things in order to effectively and efficiently pursue our purpose in Christ Jesus. Here are five stages of reviewing life based on Psalm 139:23-34.

Five stages of reviewing life

In Psalm 139, David makes a request of God in his desire to improve by praying, "Search me, O God, and know my heart; test me and know my anxious thoughts. See if there is any offensive way in me, and lead me in the way everlasting." There are actually five requests that David is making of God in this one verse: search me, know me, test me, see me, and lead me. If you will allow this analogy, David is looking to God as his "coach." He is asking God to observe him. David is not just asking God to watch him, but to closely analyze him. This is a very vulnerable step. David is opening himself up to microscopic observation, critique, and correction.

Then David requests that God know him. In this request, David is not just seeking analysis. He is asking God to become acquainted with his heart and know his desires, both good and bad, and not only know his actions, but the motives behind them. This is an even deeper unveiling by David to his God in the efforts to be "coached" in the proper manner.

David then goes into an action step by requesting that God, test him. In this stage, David is requesting that God place him in circumstances and situations that would cause David's true character to be revealed. An example of this step for us might be how we act if things don't go our way. How do we respond when people are rude to us? How do we react when someone in authority over us tells us, "No?" What do we do when we are tempted and no one is watching? How do we behave when we are placed in positions of authority over others? What do we do when we are rejected? What is our disposition when someone hurts our feelings? What if we are wrong and others bring it to our attention? These are all tests that produce results for God to see us.

God sees the real us when we face trials (refer to James 1). Eventually, what is in us will come out of us. But if we are to improve, we must undergo this testing so that God can see if there is anything in us that needs to be corrected.

And it is after all of this that David asks God to "lead me in the way everlasting." In other words, David is asking God to lead him in the direction that God would take him, which is eternity. This is a model prayer, and an excellent framework for the person who wants to review his/her race with God.

The hurdle that must be overcome here is the hurdle of pride. We use pride to cover up our shortcomings and protect ourselves from appearing weak. We use overcompensation in our success areas to mask our failures. When we place ourselves in protection mode, it becomes more difficult for us to open ourselves up to others, including God, to reveal our weaknesses.

This is quite ironic, however, when it comes to God. If you are anything like me there are times when you have convinced yourself that you can actually hide things from God as if God were a guest visiting your house and before He arrives you cram all of your junk in the back closet. The reality is that God already sees us and already knows everything about us. When we pray the prayer of David, we are not asking God literally to know us; He already knows us. We are surrendering ourselves to God, opening our closets, if you will, and giving Him the permission and authority to lead us. Said in another way, we are relinquishing our secrets and control to the leadership of God.

This is far easier to talk about than to do. However, if we ask God for the boldness and strength to pursue this step we will navigate this hurdle with swiftness and grace. Imagine you have done something you have come to regret. And this act brings you shame and embarrassment when you think about it. Interestingly, it is not simply the act that needs to be corrected (though it usually does). It is the motive behind the act. This, you may recall, is the "know me" stage of David's prayer. What was in your heart to drive you toward that action? What was the need you were attempting to meet? What was the desire you were attempting to satisfy? What was the hurt you were trying to heal?

Unchecked, you may continuously correct certain actions, but the behavior will persist until you allow God to see it and lead you to considering His way of dealing with this rather than your way, which to this point has probably not worked out for you. I can vividly recall times in my life in which I experienced sin cycles daily. I would be focused on good things, doing the right things, living faithfully, helping people, treating people well, and then, in any given moment, something would rise up in me, I would do something wrong, I would feel bad and I would end up asking, "Why does this keep happening?" You know the cycle … wash, spin, rinse, repeat. We ask the Lord to wash us of our sins by saying, "Help me, Lord." Then after doing good for a time, something happens and we begin to spin out of control. Then we are rinsed over by guilt and shame. So we ask God to wash us of our sins and so on. But now it's time to break this cycle. Unfortunately for me, I was not capable of doing this on my own. I sought out a Christian counselor who would serve as my coach and help me review the film of my life. For me I really wanted to know why I could not rid myself of the stronghold of pornography. I wanted to know why I needed attention from women who were not my wife. I wanted to understand how it could be that one moment I was having a great day and in a split second I would fall into depression and loneliness only to find myself attempting to ease that pain through indulgence in pornography or the comforting words of other women. These are examples of my sin cycles. What I learned was that, because I was raised by

It was great to learn that I was not just a lost soul who was destined to negative cycles for the rest of my life.

my mother, the words of a woman were very important to me. However, because my mother had to work so hard as a single mom to care for us and was gone from home so much of the time, I had a longing for the attention of women. This in and of itself was not necessarily all that bad. However, mix in the fact that I was a product of divorced parents and was introduced to sexual material and conduct at a very young age, this longing became a dysfunction that would lead to destructive behavior. What happened in that process was, through the help of another individual, God allowed me to be searched and known. To me this was an eye opener. It was great to learn that I was not just a lost soul who was destined to negative cycles for the rest of my life. But my next question was, now that I know this what do I do about it? Through our time together, my counselor would listen to my laments with careful analysis and a gifting that could only come from God. One session after my sharing, he sat up in his chair and with a calm but firm voice he said, "I have an assignment for you that we will discuss in our next session." What he asked me to do was to keep a notepad by my side (smartphones and tablets had not been invented yet), and every day and night document each time a temptation came over me or if I felt like I was beginning to emotionally spiral downward. I had to do this daily until our weekly meeting. Before I got halfway through the week I could see patterns. I noticed that when someone encouraged me, I performed better. I noticed when my wife was in a good mood, I felt better. When things were going well, I was more inspired. This sounds pretty basic, right? But I also noticed that if my wife was not pleased with me or spoke to me in a certain way, then I was tempted to quickly run somewhere else to find affirmation. I learned that if a stressful situation were to arise on my job that I could not control or if there was conflict with anyone for any reason that I could not resolve, I would be tempted to quickly fall into self-doubt and depression and long for immediate relief. I also noticed that if any attractive woman were to look at me and smile or give me any attention at all, I would be tempted to believe that she liked me and wanted a relationship with me. These were my tendencies that would lead to negative behavior. This was an example of reviewing the film of my life. And this film was both revealing and fascinating to me. Knowing the root of these temptations and knowing the types of things that would trigger them helped me devise a strategy to combat them.

I realize not everyone has the same challenges as mine. But everyone has challenges of some nature. Whether it is pride, anger, perfectionism, judging others, lack of self control, self-centeredness, negativity, vanity, or other issues, we all have something. What is yours and how do you deal with it?

The strategy that I employ, with God's help, is connected to the experience of my first hurdle race mentioned earlier in this chapter. That strategy includes Realizing the Walls, Recognizing the People, Retaining the Options, and Remembering the Finish Line. These elements are important in my process of conducting an effective review.

Realize the walls

You will recall my imagery of hurdles appearing as a series of walls. As a runner approaches the starting line, these walls do not go unnoticed. The whole purpose of the race is to overcome them. Likewise, in life there are walls. Sometimes, because life can be so overwhelming, we choose to ignore these walls and hope all will go well with us. This is a passive approach. However, if we want to be successful we need to first realize that these walls exist. These walls can be pride, insecurities, lack of trust or lack of connection to emotions due to past hurts, and anger, just to name a few. What are your walls? What things get you stirred up and cause you to be distracted from your purpose? Not only do we need to recognize the walls, we need to change our perspective in dealing with them. In both high school and in college, my coaches taught me something about hurdles that I never forgot. They told me that, when running a hurdle race, we need to attack the hurdles. That means that hurdlers look at hurdles as obstacles that are in the way. There are two options: we can leap over them with power or we can kick them down. I don't know about you, but I've had enough of my walls attacking me. It is time that I become the attacker. And I have made up my mind that, with God's help, I am either going to leap over them or kick them down. No longer do I see my walls as insurmountable, immovable objects. I now see them as obstacles in the way of my destiny — and anything in the way of my destiny needs to be overcome or kicked down.

What are your walls? What things get you stirred up and cause you to be distracted from your purpose?

Recognize the people

In a hurdle race, there are at least eight runners on the track. These runners all start the race at the same time and run the same number of hurdles. All of the hurdles are at the same height and have the same distance between them. In other words, you have different people running the same race. In life, we are all different, but running the same race too, and we all have hurdles to navigate. However, recognizing that there are other people navigating similar hurdles as us bears significance. First, we need to recognize that we are not alone. Some of our obstacles are frustrating and some are painful. It is easy to falsely believe that no one understands what we are going through. The reality is that, if people were honest, we would realize that our experiences are more similar than unique. Knowing that we are not alone may encourage us to know that we can successfully navigate our challenges. There are two cautions to which we need to heed when recognizing other people who are in the race of life with us. First, we need to be careful of comparing our race with others. We all navigate at a different pace and run with different styles. This means that it may take some of us longer to navigate a particular challenge in our lives than others and vice versa. Becoming overly self-critical or criticizing others for not moving through their circumstances as quickly as we believe they should is not only counterproductive, but it is not what God would do. We all need to stay in our own lanes and focus on our own races while loving others as they navigate theirs. The second caution we need to heed is to be aware of how our race impacts others. I once ran in a race where the runner in the lane next to me tripped over his hurdle and fell into my lane. This caused me to stumble and negatively impacted my race. There are times when our failures will negatively impact those around us. Though our objective is not to live our lives at the pleasure of others, as Christians we should live lives that bring life to others. We do need to be considerate of how our decisions and actions will impact others. As reflected in Romans 14:21, we don't want to do anything that causes others to stumble. We need to recognize others around us and live our lives accordingly.

> **We all need to stay in our own lanes and focus on our own race while loving others as they navigate theirs.**

Retain the options

One common trait shared by all high-performing athletes is

the drive to compete and win. Arguably, it is this drive that makes good athletes great. This type of drive does not just exist in athletes. Some have a drive to compete in the classroom, in the workplace, or in life. A drive to compete can be a great intrinsic mechanism to propel us toward success. However, this same drive can cause damage. Sometimes the lines can be blurred between when to press and when to stop. Most elite runners know when  to stop. They know that at the first sign of a muscle strain it is time to shut it down or risk more severe damage. This is a good lesson to apply to life. There are times when hitting the pause button temporarily might actually help us to focus. Unlike an actual hurdle race where stopping will cause you to lose, in the race of life, taking a moment to pray, reflect and seek guidance as we navigate our hurdles is actually sign of wisdom. Though we don't want to embrace the habit of quitting, there are times when we need to evaluate change. Here are some questions we might consider. Do I need to continue to live in the same location? Am I required to remain at the same job? Do I have to continue to hang out with the same group of people? Is it time to reevaluate some of my relationships? Do I need to reestablish some of my life goals? Do I just need a vacation? Whether or not we believe it, there are always options. One of those options is to simply stop for a moment.

Remember the finish line

The final stage of this strategy is to remember the finish line. The previous stage encourages us to retain the option to briefly stop. However, some of us might mistake pausing for stopping entirely. The purpose of a pause is to refresh, recalibrate, and be reminded of the goal. In a race, runners don't just start running

— they are looking to cross the finish line. And in each race runners run, they are attempting to run the race better than ever before. Though there are many personal goals we may establish throughout our lifetimes, there are only two that I would suggest as ultimate goals. One of the goals we pursue daily throughout our lives and the other is our "finish line." The first is found in Matthew 22:47-39 when he instructs that the greatest commandments are to love the Lord with all of your heart, soul, and mind, and to love your neighbor as you love yourself. I have found that if I set out each day to love the Lord with everything I have and everything within me then I live a powerful and meaningful life. If I love the Lord then I watch what I say and what I do. But more importantly, it is out of my love for the Lord that I will do what He has equipped me to do and go where He has instructed me to go. In other words, through Him, I learn what He has gifted me to do and will do it with all of my heart. But this can't be done by me alone. I must follow the other half of this commandment and love my neighbors as I love myself. I have to be attentive to those around me. I have to model the love of the Lord and love people as the Lord loves me. And the Lord loves me when I am doing well and when I am at my worst. The Lord loves me in spite of me so that I can learn what God's love looks like. If I pursue these as daily goals then I will run a very efficient race. The ultimate goal is reflected in Jesus' words in his parable of the talents (or gifts). In Matthew 25, Jesus tells a story of three individuals who were given money from a very rich man. The rich man informs them that he will return to see what they have done with his money. After leaving for a long time, the man returns to receive back his investment. Two of the recipients made money from his investment. The third individual hid his money and gave him back the same amount that he was given. The third individual was called wicked and lazy because he did nothing with what he was given. The moral of the story that Jesus tells, is that we are given gifts from God, and as recipients of these gifts, we are to use and increase them so that in the end when God asks us to give an account we can respond with a positive answer. But what I like the most about this story is the investor's response to the two individuals who grew their investments. He looked upon them and said, "Well done, good and faithful servants." In my life, the ultimate goal or finish line, is to get to the end of my life, having loved God with everything I have and loved others in the way God has loved me, and hear God say to me, "Well done!" This is the finish line I remember when I feel like giving up.

Remember, we all have areas that need to be revealed and corrected. We all have tendencies that need to be checked. The enemy knows this about us. The enemy watches our film. He does not have the power to make us do anything; however, he does watch our tendencies. This is what makes him the master tempter. We can only be tempted with areas that align with our desires. For example, if we hate the smell of cigarettes the enemy will not use imagery of cigarette smoke to tempt us. However, if we struggle with lust we might be amazed by how many desirable feelings and people come across our paths in our moments of weakness. Lust is just one example of the many areas with which Christians struggle. But through the power of Christ, we don't have to be on the losing end of the struggle. Knowing that you have a spiritual adversary that watches your tendencies and seeks to cause you to fall, wouldn't you rather give your weaknesses to God who can keep you from falling? With God's help and the help of others, regularly review and run your race of life with purpose and efficiency.

LIFE QUESTIONS

1. What are your personal challenges?

2. What hesitations do you have about reviewing the film of your life?

3. Who can you ask to help you review your film?

4. In what ways can you enhance your love of God and others?

5. What do you believe your love of God and others will reveal and how will it sustain your focus on your life purpose?

PRACTICAL STEPS

Step 1: Declare change.

You will read exhortations like this multiple times throughout this book. If you want change in your life you must make a personal declaration from your heart. Going back and revisiting things in your past can be an incredibly difficult process that might send you into a flurry of emotions. In the process of going back and reviewing the film of your life there will be moments you will be tempted to abandon the process. When times get tough through the process, remember why you desire to change. Remember the defeat you experienced as a result of bad habits. But also keep at the forefront of your mind the triumph of the freedom you will experience when you establish new habits and practices in your life.

Step 2: Begin the search process.

Now that you have made up your mind, start this journey. A good place to start is with God. We discussed the process found in Psalm 139. This step requires you to establish some prayer and reflection time as you ask God to show your reflection. The word of God, like the Scripture referenced, coupled with prayer and reflection, will begin to reveal areas that may need spiritual attention. If you haven't tried this before it can seem strange. But the idea of mindfulness, reflection, and journaling is not a foreign concept. My encouragement is to invite God into the process and see what happens. Consult a pastor or someone who has experienced a Christian journey to see if you would like to explore this step further.

Step 3: Beware of over-exaggeration.

As you review the film of your past experiences there is an important message to understand. You are not perfect. However, you are not terrible either. Though I am far from perfect, I have matured in my manhood and my faith. Reflecting back on bad things I have done in my past, I am tempted to overly criticize how bad I was. The reality is that I may have done some things that were bad, I was not a bad person. When you look back on your past with honesty, you may find that you have done wrong or even terrible things. Remember what you have done does not define who you are. You are a creation of God. You were created in the image and likeness of Him. As a created being of God, you are an amazing and dynamic individual. You have a brilliance that cannot be defined. The question is, do you believe and behave like it? Avoid the temptation of thinking everything is perfect in your life and you do not need of help. But also avoid the temptation of believing that you are so broken that you are beyond repair.

Step 4: Find a good coach.

Remember we cannot win this race by ourselves. Every successful martial artist has had an instructor. Every successful doctor has had professors. Every successful entrepreneur has had mentors. Every successful athlete has had coaches. If you want to be successful in school look for a good team of coaches (e.g., teachers and tutors). If you want to be successful in business look for a good business coach. If you want to be successful in your thinking, look for a good mind coach (e.g., counselor or pastor). The point here is, if you want to be successful in any area look for those who have achieved success and allow them to walk with you. This is especially true of your faith walk. If you haven't already done so, find a good coach today.

PERSONAL PRAYERS/REFLECTIONS

REVISE THE PLAN

"Do you not know that in a
race all the runners run, but
only one gets the prize? Run in
such a way as to get the prize.
Everyone who competes in the
games goes into strict training."

—1 Corinthians 9:23-25

"All success is, really, is having
a predetermined plan and
carrying it out successfully over
a long period of time."

— Harvey Mackay

Though I was a runner in high school and college I never ran long distances. As I got older I began jogging for exercise, but still never ran more than a couple of miles. One day while walking through a shopping mall, I saw an advertisement for a charity 5K run for a very popular organization and a truly noble cause. For some strange reason something in me said, "Why not. What do I have to lose?" So I signed up for the run, thinking how cool it would be to run in my first 5K. Then I remembered that a 5K is 3.1 miles, which is a distance I had never run before except for a couple of times on a treadmill while listening to music and not paying much attention. Therefore I started going to the gym to intentionally prepare for this run. I ran on the treadmill up to three times a week in my attempt to get ready. I got to a point where I was running at least 3.1 miles every time I stepped into the gym. In my mind, my every intention was to finish the race. As the day of the 5K approached, I mentioned to a co-worker, who happened to be a cross-country coach, that I was running in my first 5K. He responded, "Man, that is so cool. Do you want me to run with you?" I thought that was a great idea, however, I didn't want to look like a loser in front of a guy who could easily run five to ten miles a day in his sleep. He said, "Don't worry man. I'm just going out there to support you as a running buddy and have some fun." Having him as a running partner was probably the best thing that could have happened. I will share why in a moment. But let's fast forward to the day of the race. The big day arrived and there were easily a couple of thousand runners at the iconic Southern California stadium. There were people there from all walks of life. Every age, from babies in strollers to elderly people, was represented. Athletically, some people were simply there to have fun and support a worthy cause, while others were there to compete. As it turned out, this particular event was officially timed and recognized as an official race. Serious runners who ran fast enough times could qualify for higher profile competitive running events. Now remember, my goal was to run and finish the race without stopping. This is where the apostle Paul's writing in 1 Corinthians 9:23-25 comes in. The first statement he makes is, "… all of the runners run, but only one gets the prize." As previously mentioned, in my race, some were competing and others were not. However, of all the serious competitors that day, only one would be declared the winner. Yet, there is a deeper meaning that Paul is conveying in this text through the analogy of a race. What he is actually referring to is the race of life. And what he is conveying is not that there is only one winner, but that all runners who run the race in a proper manner can be winners. He goes on to say, "Run in such a way as to win the prize." In this statement he tells us the attitude and passion we should have as runners in this race. If we are going to run then we need to run to win. In other words, if we are going to live then we need to live in such a way that will lead us to a victorious life. Now that just makes sense to me. How many times do we find ourselves living lives of such habit and routine that we feel like the proverbial hamster running on an endless wheel to nowhere? How often do we find ourselves, tired and stressed out wondering what was actually accomplished. At what point are we going to decide, enough is enough! If we are going to live, then why not live it up? Now I'm not talking about the type of living it up that leads us right back to regret, hopelessness, and emptiness. I'm talking about living life to our maximum capacity knowing that we made the most of each day. So how do we do this? In the above text, Paul continues, "Everyone who competes in the games goes into strict training." You will recall how I prepared to run the 5K race and how I increased the intensity of my workouts so I would be in the best condition to finish. Can you imagine the level of training high-level athletes submit themselves to when preparing for the Olympic Games? One world-class swimmer shared in an interview that his training was so intense that he burned 10,000 calories per day. To give you context, an hour-long cycling or spin class will burn up to 1,000 calories. For athletes who are preparing for the Olympic Games, intense training is a lifestyle. In fact, many of them have sponsors because training for such a high level becomes a full-time job. And this training entails more

> **If we are going to live, then we need to live in such a way that will lead us to a victorious life.**

than working out. It requires a disciplined diet, rest, and sacrificing certain pleasures in life that would impede the ability to win. Now keeping this in mind, remember Paul is talking about the game of life. The strict training that he is referring to consists of discipline. Like the Olympic athlete, if we want to be in the best position to win the race of life, we have to go into strict training. Stated differently, a victorious life requires discipline and continuous training. In fact it would be quite arrogant to think otherwise. To believe we can truly be great at something without investing the time or effort would be quite narcissistic. So what does strict training look like? If we want to be at our best, we need to go into training physically, spiritually, and emotionally with the same passion as a high-level athlete. In Mark 12:30 Jesus says that the greatest commandment is that we love the Lord with all of our heart, soul, mind, and strength. This means we need to love God with everything that we have. All of our passion, our being, our emotions, and our physical strength should be dedicated to God. As Jesus spoke the words, he was referencing the words of Moses spoken in Deuteronomy 6. Now it is important to know that this commandment comes with promises. According to Moses, if we pursue God in this manner then it will go well with us: we will increase greatly, we will prosper, and we will be alive. Now that's the life I want to have. But it doesn't stop here. This brings us full circle back to where we started with Paul. If you continue reading Paul's words in 1 Corinthians 9, after he tells us that everyone who competes goes into strict training, he continues by expressing that some people pursue a crown that won't last. But real victory is in pursuing a crown that lasts forever. So what are crowns that don't last? Before we answer this question, let's look at the context here. Remember, Paul is giving us imagery of the Olympic Games. During the time of this writing, the winner of every event would have a wreath placed on his head representing a crown of victory. This was, and still is, a great achievement. However, the crown was made of leaves, which eventually die. In other words, as great an achievement as it was to receive the crown of victory, that crown doesn't last. Relating this imagery to life, a crown can represent any material item that we might count as an achievement that doesn't last. How many people do you know today that pursue crowns that don't last?

Fine clothing, nice cars, beautiful homes, nice furniture, and other material items are wonderful to have, but they don't last. I have driven through neighborhoods in various cities where the houses are at least fifty years old and the areas are run-down. When I drove through these areas I would wonder what these homes must have looked like when they were brand-new. Can you imagine being the homeowner of a brand-new house? Well, in fifty years that house would no longer be brand-new and, in some cases, the neighborhood may no longer be desirable. In fact, since then some of these homes have been demolished and rebuilt, and others have been abandoned. The point is, today many of the homes I viewed in certain neighborhoods no longer held the value they once did. And think of the investment the original homeowners must have made to acquire those dream houses. But let's take this a little deeper. We pursue many things in life that give us satisfaction, and may even be counted as great accomplishments, but do not last forever. I had the opportunity to work at a Christian prep school in Southern California. As an administrator, I made significant contributions to that school, which helped build the school's reputation and allowed it to become an academic competitor among the prominent schools in the area. Because of my and my colleagues' efforts, many of the school's students obtained admissions into reputable colleges. I also had the opportunity to coach two sports, one of which I was a head coach and lead in our high school conference and got our athletes recognized. These were great accomplishments that were at one time celebrated. However, if you were to go to that campus today, very few people (if any) would know who I am or have any knowledge of my contributions. These were all crowns that did not last. That is not to say that we should not strive for excellence. And I am not trying to imply that just because people don't remember us that our contributions are meaningless. What I am saying, and what the apostle Paul is saying in his text, is that the significance of certain achievements, or crowns, will not last forever. In other words, I should strive to be a person of excellence who makes significant contributions and earns achievements in life, but those should not be the end result. Each achievement or victory is a mile marker to our destination or finish line, if you will. The crown that is being referred to here is eternal life, which ironically is neither earned nor achieved, but we will address this later. Before we reach the end of our lives on this earth, however, we should live lives of victorious mile markers and meaningful contributions. This is what Jesus refers to as abundant life. But to do this, we need to review our lives and revise our plan for success. I believe if we truly want to be successful, we need to get **R.E.A.L.**

> **Before we reach the end of our lives on this earth, we want to live lives of victorious mile markers and meaningful contributions.**

Remember the goal

Throughout our lifetime we will find ourselves setting, and sometimes accomplishing many different types of goals. Some of us have set educational goals that we desired to complete, e.g., the requirements to earn a diploma, degree, license, or certification. Some of us have set out to accomplish financial goals in which we desired to either build savings or purchase something special. We may have sought to improve our physical or emotional health by setting fitness, nutrition, or wellness goals. And then there are those New Year's resolutions in which some of us make vows for improvement or success at the beginning of a given year. There are many more examples, but one thing all of these have in common is that sometimes we meet them and sometimes we don't. But the most important common denominator is the fact that once we accomplish these goals, it is only a matter of time that we find ourselves asking, "Now what?" Now that I have the diploma or certificate on the wall, what am I going to do? Now that I have made the purchase or built my savings to a comfortable level, what's next? Now that I have reached my health goals or arrived at a better emotional place, what is my next challenge? The reality is goal setting and achievement can, and should be, never-ending until the day we die. But if we keep asking ourselves, "What's next?" then what's the point? I would like to suggest one approach that answers this question and will clarify the ultimate finish line for our lives. I propose that we seek to understand and pursue spiritual goals. Now the first step in this process is to believe in spirituality and an eternal existence. For me, the day I made the decision to believe in Jesus Christ and to align my purposes to the Scriptures in the Bible, my life was never the same. The first step of my process relates to John 3:16 in the Bible in which it says that God loved the world so much that he gave is one and only son (Jesus) and whoever believes in him will have eternal life. This was important to me as it caused me to realize that my life is beyond me and what I personally achieve or acquire for my satisfaction. Life is so much bigger than that. And I am a living witness that though my spiritual life in Christ does not make me perfect, my ultimate goal is perfectly clear. I love the words of Paul written in 2 Timothy 4:7-8 as he was approaching the last days of his life when he said, "I have fought the good fight, I have finished the race, I have kept the faith. Now there is in store for me the crown of righteousness, which the Lord, the righteous Judge, will award to me on that day; and not only to me, but also to all who have longed for his appearing." I believe there is eternal life waiting at the end of this race called life. And I want to know that my life was one of fighting for myself and others, striving to bring inspiration to this world by connecting people to something greater than themselves, and holding onto my faith, which will sustain me to the end and help others to do the same. How about you? Who

> **Goal setting and achievement can, and should be, never-ending until the day we die.**

have you been living for? Where have your goals led you? If you find there is still something missing, consider taking the step that I did. Now I mentioned earlier that this step toward eternal life is not earned. God gives us this gift by simply accepting Christ. However, we all have lives to live and that is where the spiritual goal setting comes in. When Paul says that he has kept the faith, it means that he has lived a life that aligned with the Scriptures. Though it wasn't easy — hence his expression of fighting the good fight — he did what was right by God until the end of his days. Along with our personal, physical, and financial goals, we need to establish spiritual goals for our lives. Spiritual goals are the action steps we commit to take that will make us stronger in our walk of faith and bring us closer to God. Again, I can attest to the fact that, when my faith walk is stronger, not only do I live with a clear conscience, but I am a greater benefit to those around me. Now this next statement I make with caution, but boldness. Because of my faith, God has allowed me to experience an abundant life. No, I am neither rich and famous nor have I amassed numerous possessions, but my wife and I continue to enjoy marriage after more than 23 years, my children (who are now adults) enjoy our family time together, I am successful in my workplace, and God has blessed me to lead a ministry that is impacting lives. I am not bragging, but giving my personal testimonial. And just like the infomercials we see on television, I call it my testimonial because there was a before and an after. Before my faith walk, I was living for me, neglecting my family and still toiling for success. After developing my faith walk, faithfulness became more important to me than success. The fact that I happen to experience success in my life is, quite frankly, an added bonus. By remembering my eternal goal and focusing on my faith as well as my other goals, I am beginning to realize more and more what true abundant life is all about.

Enhance your training

There is not much argument against the old adage, "Practice makes perfect." Though there are a few exceptions, we know that if we practice something enough we will get better at it. We have already discussed how high-level athletes go through intense training. But even with amateur athletes who are not standouts, they will improve if they continue to practice. In school students practice by doing educational activities in the classroom and homework assignments. While not every student is a straight-A student, those who practice will improve. The person who finds a hobby or is interested in a particular craft, even if they never become highly acclaimed, with practice gets better. One of my hobbies is playing golf. Now I will be the first to admit that I am not very good. Most of the time when I hit the ball, I hope it will go where I want it to go. However, most of the time it doesn't. The truth is, though I have been casually and sporadically playing golf for many years, I have never taken the time to have golf lessons. Therefore, I am fully aware that I have weak fundamentals. With weak fundamentals come bad habits. Bad habits lead to weak performance. Hence we are back to my original statement that I am not very good at golf. Let's apply this concept to life. There were certain aspects of my life that I was not very good at, and consequently I even hurt people because of my poor performance. As I was developing during my teen years I was very confused. I grew up with a blended family. I have an older brother on my mother's side and two older brothers and an older sister on my father's side. I am the only child born to both my mother and father together. When I was a young child, my parents got divorced and my siblings on my father's side lived with their mother. Therefore, for most of my childhood years, I grew up in a single-parent home. When my brother on my mother's side turned eighteen he moved out of our house. At that time, I was about eleven years old. Because my mother had to fulfill the roles of both mother and father, she worked many hours and I was at home alone much of the time. Just prior to my 14th birthday, my father died of lung cancer. This is a very brief and superficial summary of my circumstances; however, I had many other experiences, both physical and emotional, that were quite painful. Even though my father taught me great lessons while he was alive, and my mother instilled strength and core values that serve as pillars for me to this day, my foundation was flawed and I acquired many bad habits along the way. My mother was very polished and quite dignified. Therefore, I was raised knowing how to speak to people and how to present myself. If you were to ask many of my classmates in junior high and high school they would probably remember me as a good guy, good student, and decent athlete. I flew under the radar well. The reality was, I was quite lonely, quite lost and sought to find significance in sports and girls. As I grew older I engaged in many bad habits. But remember, I knew how to fly under the radar. I was not into drugs, nor was alcohol my thing, but early on I was introduced to pornography and I was hooked. Furthermore, I was trained by men in my life at an early age on how to be a ladies' man. That's just a sanitized phrase for womanizing. As a teen, if I wasn't engaged in sexual activity through pornography, I was engaged in sexual activity with girls. Why am I telling you all of this? It is in no way to dishonor my parents or family. It is in no way to disparage my upbringing. It is to share with you the truth of my life that there were certain things that were trained into me and I went even deeper into bad practices and habits on my own. However, once I committed to and grew in my faith, I learned that if I was trained in bad habits, I could be retrained in good ones. Romans 12:2 says, "Do not be conformed to the pattern of this world, but be transformed by the renewing of your mind." I reached a point in my life where enough was enough. I was tired of hurting women, I was tired of viewing women as objects, I was tired of living in loneliness, I was tired of being controlled by my impulses and I was tired of living a defeated life in the shadows. It was time to enhance my training. It was time to renew my thinking, my approaches, my philosophies and my actions. How did I do this? First, by recognizing that I had problems and needed to change. Then by seeking help through Christian counseling and the leadership of other men who were living lives of integrity who could walk with me on my journey. But this was not a one-shot deal. It wasn't a one session or one "conversation with the guys" solution. This was a long process of changing habits. For example, I changed

> **Once I committed to and grew in my faith, I learned that if I was trained in bad habits, I could be retrained in good ones.**

the images I would allow myself to take in through movies, television, magazines, and the internet. This was one of the areas that my struggle began and was part of the foundation of my poor thinking. Therefore, I needed to destroy that foundation and build a new one. Not to sound too spiritual, but for me I had to make the Scriptures of the Bible my truth and learn and walk in those teachings. This required strict discipline and changes in my thinking and actions. Does this mean I became perfect? Absolutely not. But the enhancement of my training led to changes of habits. Though I still had strong temptations, my attachments to pornography and self-gratification are gone. And, yes, I made mistakes along the way, but my heart and my time to recovery has changed. I have been set free from those things that made me feel like a prisoner in chains. And this training can't stop. One thing I learned is, without discipline, I can easily slide back into poor thinking and bad habits. Again, I'm still not perfect, but I am free.

Acquire training partners

Many people make New Year's resolutions in which they pledge to pursue life goals for the upcoming year. Among these resolutions is the goal to exercise and pursue health and fitness. This is great news each year for fitness centers and health clubs. There is no shortage of television commercials and special deals to join health clubs at the beginning of each year. But one thing people in the fitness profession will agree on is that it is good to have a workout partner. A workout partner is not simply there to work out. A workout partner will hold you accountable to go to the gym when you least feel like it. A workout partner can also encourage you to push farther, work harder, and accomplish more than you might on your own.

> **I have been set free from those things that made me feel like a prisoner in chains.**

Ecclesiastes 4:9 says, "Two are better than one, because they have a good return for their labor." In other words, two people can accomplish more together than one person can accomplish on his or her own. Working together, two or more people when moving toward the same goal can also work more efficiently. In the story of my 5K race, I shared how I invited a colleague to run with me. Though he didn't actually train with me, he was with me throughout the race, encouraging me along the way. There were times during that race when I felt like stopping. However, my running buddy, who knew I was capable of continuing, would encourage me to keep going. Even though he could have breezed through the race, he slowed down and stayed with me. He would regularly check in and ask me how I was doing. He would also sing and crack jokes while we were running. I thought, "This dude is singing and cracking jokes while I'm barely surviving out here!" There were times I wanted to ask him to be quiet and let me focus, but looking back I realized that he was trying to distract me from focusing on how tired I was and loosen me up so I could enjoy the run. These are all great lessons for our life pursuits. Now when I tell this story of my running buddy to others and suggest how it is better to have a workout partner, there are those who disagree with me. But when I suggest that we all need help dealing with our personal issues and need people in our lives to guide us, walk with us, and hold us accountable there is resistance. Is it pride? Do we want people to stay out of our personal business? Are we too embarrassed to reveal our weaknesses? One of the many things I have learned on my journey is that I cannot make it on my own. I am grateful to have a wife who walks strong in her faith and pursues Christ with all of her heart. She is also someone who will not allow me to quit in my faith because we are in this race together. But I am also blessed to have an accountability partner. This is a man who is strong in his faith, is doing his best by his family, and living a life of integrity. Again, this is not a perfect man, but we share our imperfections with each other and encourage each other to continue to do the right things. We talk every week and share our good, bad, and ugly with each other. He won't allow me to quit, and I won't allow him to give up. We are running this race together. And I can honestly tell you that I run far more efficiently with him than I would without him. I also have other men in my life that are like brothers to me. We encourage each other, inspire each other, pray for each other, and know that we can call on each other in times of need. These are not just any guys. These are men who are successful in their races of life that I can run with and be motivated to continue on my journey. Who are your "training partners?" How often do you "train" together? How has your life been more effective with them in it? If you don't have any training partners, what is stopping you? Two are indeed better than one.

Listen to your coaches

I will never forget the words of my college track coach. Here I was this eighteen-year-old kid who thought he was special, which is ironic because I was not a stellar athlete. One day the athletes and I were on the track and the coach told us we were going to practice a particular aspect of the race. While everyone was working on the drill, I walked up to the coach and said, "Hey Coach, I already know how to do this." His response to me was both humbling and embarrassing. He said, "You don't know how to do this because I haven't taught you yet." What my coach was saying was that you may know how to do this your way, but now it's time to learn my way. This has become a lifelong mantra for me. I have a number of life coaches whom I follow. As clichéd as this may sound, my first coach is God. I have learned many things throughout my life, but I have constantly asked the question, "Is this God's

As cliché as this may sound, my first coach is God.

way?" There are three ways I can tell if I am doing something God's way. First, the Scriptures found in the Bible will teach me what God says and how He operates. If I ever want to speak or act in a way that would please God, I can always test what I am doing by the principles found in the Scriptures. Secondly, every Christian is given the gift of the Holy Spirit. Some might say the Holy Spirit is like your conscience, but the Holy Spirit is much more. John 14:26 says, "… the Holy Spirit, whom the Father will send in my name, will teach you all things and will remind you of everything I have said to you." The Holy Spirit is a teacher and a guide who helps us in all areas. I guess you can say the Holy Spirit is our spiritual coach, inside of us, who guides us. I have been saved from poor outcomes many times by listening to this spiritual voice inside of me. Likewise, I have benefited greatly by listening to the instructions of this spiritual voice who has guided me to do the right things. The third way to know that I am doing things God's way is to surround myself with other people who are following God. If I start to behave in a manner that is contradictory to my faith, it is helpful to have others who notice and are bold enough to let me know that I need to make corrections. These people are important as we are all running this race together. Aside from God, I have other coaches who help me to be my spiritual best. I have spiritual mentors to whom I can turn to in times of need who will give me the guidance I need. However, I have one spiritual mentor who I speak to about once per month who encourages me and instructs me through many aspects of my faith walk. This man is a true coach to me and is not afraid to check me on certain things and who constantly builds me up through affirming words about me. But it is important to know that this coaching only works because I do what he says. Now if any of my coaches from my youth read this book they will be surprised to know that I listen to my coach now because this was not the case in my younger days. I was the kid who thought only certain people could teach me. On top of that, I still wanted to do things my way. This led to me to personal frustration and being so beneath my potential that as I got older I had many regrets to deal with. But today, I realize the value of coaches. The wisdom of those who have gone before me and have made accomplishments in areas I am currently navigating now is incredibly invaluable. My current coach, whom I refer to as my Pastor, is such an important person in my life, words cannot explain how blessed I am as a husband, father, and leader to have his guidance. Therefore, strengthen your connection to God who is your first coach by doing things His way, and find at least one good spiritual mentor who can guide you through your journey and, I promise, your life will never be the same.

LIFE QUESTIONS

1. What crowns have you been pursuing that will not last?

2. In what area of your life do you need strict training?

3. List three goals that you can pursue over the next three months (one spiritual, one physical, or one mental).

PRACTICAL STEPS

Remember if you want to revise your plan you have to get REAL.

Step 1: Remember the goal.

There are immediate goals, and there is the ultimate goal of our lives. The ultimate goal for Christians is to reach the finish line of life having done right by God, family, friends, community, and self. As previously mentioned, we are commanded to love God and love our neighbors as we love ourselves. With that in mind, we need to regularly establish goals for our faith and health in order to love God with everything we have. And we need to establish goals for strengthening our relationships with others as well as serving others in our faith community and our surrounding communities. This is how we love others. Focusing on our goals allows us to remember why we are doing what we are doing. Getting inspired to make positive life changes is great. Beginning the journey of starting new practices and habits is wonderful. But there will come a time when challenges hit and you question why you ever began this journey in the first place. When things in life get tough, and you find it would be easier to go backward, remembering your goal will keep you focused on moving forward.

Step 2: Enhance your training.

Once you have established goals, it's time to put them into practice. Remember, practice makes us better. Continued practice also creates good habits. When we establish a consistent study routine in school we create study habits. When we choose to eat the right foods on a consistent basis we are establishing healthy eating habits. In other words, if we want to change we need to train ourselves to consistently do the right things. The key word here is consistently. In what areas of your life do you need to increase your consistency? Is it through study and prayer to strengthen your faith? Is it through your service? Do you have bad habits that need to be converted into good habits? Locate these areas and enhance your training.

Step 3: Acquire training partners.

In school, teachers encourage students to have study partners. In the gym, people are encouraged to have training partners. Likewise in life, we need to have people who pursue lives of faith and success in healthy ways. It is important that we make an honest assessment of who we are spending our time with as we walk through life. The people with whom we surround ourselves could have a strong impact on how we think, how we make decisions, how we navigate circumstances and, ultimately, who we become. The people we select for our inner circle become our life training partners. In evaluating this circle ask yourself these questions: What am I learning from my circle? Who am I becoming because of my circle? In the last twelve months has my circle aided in my spiritual, physical, emotional, career and life growth? Make sure you honestly evaluate these questions and acquire the right training partners for your life.

Step 4: Listen to your coaches.

We will never reach a point in our lives where we have nothing left to learn. I have been blessed to earn a bachelor's degree, two master's degrees and two doctorate degrees. Some might find this impressive. But through all of this education the one thing that I have learned is how much I still don't know. Having expertise in one area does not make you an expert in all areas. In fact, if you don't continue to learn you will even lose your expertise. Therefore, if we want to be successful we need to have good coaches in our lives. Who are your coaches? Just as we need to choose good training partners, we also need to select good coaches. A good coach is someone who doesn't just have knowledge, they can also demonstrate current success in the area in which you have need. Be careful of coaches who don't have current success records. Find a coach that can help you address the areas that you that you have indicated above, which need attention. However, having a coach will mean very little if you don't listen to and follow the advice. If you want to achieve success in your life identify and listen to your coaches.

PERSONAL PRAYERS/REFLECTIONS

RUN WITH PASSION

"Not that I have already obtained all this, or have already arrived at my goal, but I press on to take hold of that for which Christ Jesus took hold of me. Brothers and sisters, I do not consider myself yet to have taken hold of it. But one thing I do: Forgetting what is behind and straining toward what is ahead, I press on toward the goal to win the prize for which God has called me heavenward in Christ Jesus."

— Philippians 3:12-14

"There is no passion to be found playing small — in settling for a life that is less than the one you are capable of."

— Nelson Mandela

Years ago after one of my "falls" I met with one of my mentors who was a long-time, well-respected pastor in his community. I shared with him that I had fallen and expressed to him the guilt and shame that I was carrying as a result of letting so many people down, especially God. He told me a story that I will never forget.

> *"Son, I remember when I was young and played on a football team. I really thought I was something. During one game in particular I made a huge mistake and the coach pulled me out of the game. As I stood on the sideline, I knew I wasn't going to play anymore and all I could think about is the mistake I made. Then the coach called my name and said, 'Get back in there!' When I got back in that game I played harder than I ever played and gave it all that I had. One of my teammates approached me and asked me what had gotten into me. I told him, 'Coach gave me another chance.'"*

After he finished his story he said to me, "Son, God has given you another chance. Now get back in the game!" These words on the heels of my failure meant the world to me. Here was another coach who saw me in my fallen state and in his own words admonished me to, "Get up!" The difference this time was that I refused to stay down. Instead, after hearing the exhortation of my mentor, I vowed to give God everything I had and, as clichéd as it may sound, to live each day as if it were my last day on earth.

This passion is reflected in the words of the apostle Paul in his letter to the people of Philippi. As a leader, Paul shares his strategy for running with passion in Philippians 3:13-14. First he confesses that he does not always get it right nor has he already arrived at his goal. This honesty is a wonderful trait of a leader. Sometimes we see leaders who are older or more experienced and think we could never be like them. On the other hand, we sometimes see leaders who act like they have already, "arrived" but their unconfessed flaws get exposed and we see them for who they really are. Not Paul. He gives it to us straight, but he tells us how he moves forward. He tells us that the way he moves forward is to forget what is behind and strain toward what is ahead. Forgetting what is behind means to forget our past negative experiences. It is important to know that Paul had every reason to give up. As an apostle of Jesus Christ, in an area where the leaders wanted rid the earth of all people who promoted Jesus' teachings, he was rejected by his own people, imprisoned, beaten , and left for dead. But after all of this, he shares how he forgot what was behind him or what he experienced in his past. How can you forget being beaten and imprisoned? Let's bring this into context today. How do we forget our past negative experiences? Does the person who was bullied as a child simply forget about it? Does the person who was abused supposed to act as if it never happened? Does the person who experienced tragedy expect to eliminate the memory and move on? The answer is, "No!" Forgetting what is behind means to not fixate on the past. As mentioned in previous chapters, we do not simply get over the negative experiences in our lives. We acknowledge them and deal with them appropriately so we can move forward in a healthy manner. We need to deal with our problems so we can move forward, and once we do so we need to stop making our problems our focus. As Paul suggests, we need to strain toward what is ahead. The reason why moving ahead with our lives can sometimes be a strain is because we are so accustomed to focusing on what is behind us. It is a natural tendency. How many times have you been stuck in traffic on one side of the freeway because of an accident on the other side of the freeway? As you get closer to the accident on the other side,

We do not simply get over the negative experiences in our lives. We acknowledge them and deal with them appropriately so we can move forward in a healthy manner.

you ask why is everyone slowing down traffic on this side when there is nothing in front of us? You begin to get angry about your wasted time as people are impeding traffic to see the accident on the other side, only to catch yourself doing the same thing? Sometimes we are so distracted by situations in our lives around us. But we are most hindered by focusing on things in our past that keep us from moving forward. But Paul continues his strategy for success with one last step as he shares his motive. His goal is to win the prize of his calling in Christ. In other words, his ultimate goal is to passionately live out the calling of his life until he reaches Heaven.

Like Paul, I have not arrived yet nor am I perfect in any way. I have not achieved great fame nor accumulated great fortune. However, I have learned to move my focus from my past and strain forward toward the pursuit of my purpose. I have learned to live life with passion, hope, inspiration, and purpose. And most of all, I have confidence that everything I do is within God's calling on my life and toward His will for my life. Though discouraging thoughts come into my mind and reminders of the horrible things I have done in my past try to haunt me, I have learned to press through them and shift my focus toward my future. I now run with passion. How do we run with this type of passion? How do we navigate all of the hurdles of life that constantly get in our way? Hurdles can be an impediment to a runner or a runner can develop a strategy to swiftly and passionately overcome them. With this in mind, I would like to share seven strategies for overcoming the hurdles to success.

Know your purpose

You will notice there are two hurdles to success before the race actually begins. The first is preparation. Just like anything else, how we prepare can determine how successful we might be. If we want to successfully navigate the first hurdle, we must know where the hurdle is. Sometimes we run tirelessly without purpose and vision and find ourselves not accomplishing anything significant. For me, this step required clarifying the vision for my life and I could only do this by hearing from God. This begs two questions. How can we clarify our vision? And how can we hear from God? I will answer these questions in reverse order. We can hear from God in numerous ways, but each requires having a relationship with Him. This goes beyond simply saying we believe in God through Christ, but actually following Him. According to Jesus in John 8:31, if we hold onto His teachings we are truly His disciples. A disciple is one who follows the teachings of another. Therefore, it is foundational for us to follow the teachings of Christ if we want to have the ability to hear from

God. The teachings of Christ are found in the Bible, through Christian churches and Bible teachers, and through others who are followers of Christ with us. Now some of you will say, "I know this already." And I will offer this gentle reminder from James 1:22, which implores us to not just be hearers of the word, but to actually do what it says. Even the strongest followers of Christ get distracted by life circumstances and lose our direction from time to time. As I run this spiritual race, hearing from God is critical because it informs the next step which is clarifying the vision. It is God who gives me purpose and vision for my life. It is God who gives me direction for my journey. Therefore, I have to consult with God through prayer, be attentive as I look for spiritual direction, and take steps to move toward that vision. As I was seeking to clarify the vision for my life, one of my prayers to God was to give me the eyes to see. This was a request to God to help me see anything that would inform me of my vision and purpose. Through this process, I was reminded of my spiritual gifts. If you don't know your spiritual gifts consult a leader in your church community or seek a Christian spiritual gifts survey online. Two of my top spiritual gifts are discipleship (or teaching) and leadership. Secondly, I asked God to show me my heart's desire or passion. I am passionate about teaching in any context. I have taught classes in high schools, a Bible college, and universities. I have coached high school varsity sports. And I have conducted workshops for conferences around the country. I could do these things all day. As for leadership, I enjoy working with teams, establishing team mission, values, and goals, and leading teams toward accomplishing them. From this, God gave me the eyes to see my life mission, which resulted in my crafting a life mission statement. My life mission statement is to equip, encourage, and empower people to have an impact on this world. Once God allowed me to see this mission, I learned three important principles. First, anything I do in the form of occupation or ministry that is outside of my mission will not bring me fulfillment. This does not mean that I will never work outside of these areas, but I am aware of the lack of excitement I experience when I do. Second, knowing my mission will allow me to carefully choose what I spend my time doing. Third, knowing my gifts and my passion allow me to know where I will have the greatest impact. The last important aspect of God's vision for me is to realize that I live to satisfy His, not my own. Therefore, I need to continually ask God to show me where He wants me to serve out my mission. We need to regularly stop and honestly ask if we are running the right race, in the right place, and at the right time. This is an important foundational process to pursuing your purpose.

Don't lose the race before you start

This is the second hurdle to success that we encounter before the race begins. The words we speak to ourselves can have either a positive or negative impact on what we believe. Philippians 4:8 tells us to think on things that are true, noble, right, pure, lovely, admirable, excellent, or praiseworthy. This is not a simple power of positive thinking message. This is a spiritual truth. The things we think on are what we will gravitate toward and walk in. When I contemplate the way I speak to myself, there is no question of how greatly that impacts my thinking and decision-making. There are times I catch myself as I wake up in the morning constantly saying things like, "I'm so tired," "I don't feel well," and "I wish I could stay home today." It is no wonder that those were the days that I took longer to get into a positive rhythm. The truth is that any day that I wake up is a day of purpose, a day that I get the opportunity to make a difference, and a day that I get to be a light in the world. But let's take this concept a little further. What is our thinking as we approach an opportunity? There are times when opportunities present themselves and the self-talk begins. Have you ever said things like, "I'm not ready," "There's no way I can do that," or "Last time I tried this it didn't work?" Or have you ever been in a season of life where you were just tired, felt worn down and had no spiritual gas left in your tank? Think of the words we say to ourselves during those times. Were they positive or negative? Will they cause us

> **The words we speak to ourselves can have either a positive or negative impact on what we believe.**

to remain stagnant or inspire us to get up and move forward? In my story of the race where I fell it was my track coach who admonished me to get up. However, he yelled those words to me multiple times as I lay there defeated. Though I cannot recall specifically what I was saying to myself during that moment, I can imagine I was thinking about disappointment, defeat, loss, and embarrassment. I was probably envisioning my season and my chances of moving forward coming to an end. But there came a moment when, even though my coach's words were in my ears, I had to make the decision to get up. Though this was one moment in time many years ago, God has shown me a life lesson that I will never forget. There comes a time in a moment of defeat and discouragement that I have to tell myself to get up! I have to remember who I am based on the word of God. I have to remember the purpose to which God has called me. I have to remember the others around me who need life, light, hope, love, and encouragement in Christ. I have to remember that this life is not about me, but about what I have to do to give inspiration to others. It is when we think on these true, noble, right, pure, lovely, admirable, excellent, and praiseworthy things that we are encouraged to speak life and live life on purpose.

> **I have to remember that this life is not about me, but about what I am to do to give inspiration to others.**

Go!

Now that our vision is clear and our mindset is in a positive frame, it is time to start this new phase of our race. But how do we get started? I am reminded of the words of a popular slogan that gave everyone the imperative to "Just do it!" Again, if you have already navigated the first two hurdles, there is nothing stopping you from this hurdle. In fact, you should have the momentum of hope and inspiration once you approach this hurdle. I recently attended a university commencement ceremony in which the keynote speaker offered a simple, but powerful suggestion. She said, "Thinking about doing something is not doing it ... doing it is doing it." She went on to give the example that if one desires to write a book, the desire will not get it written, the conceptualization will not get it written, the creating of an outline will not get it written, nor will the establishing of a timeline get it written. Though all of these processes are important, only the writing of the book will get the book written. If I want a new job, the research of job openings and the mining through desirable position descriptions will not get me the job. At a certain point I must take action to apply and meet with people who are hiring to get the job. If I want to start a business, at a certain point I need to take the steps to establish the business and actually begin the work. If I want to establish or begin working in a ministry, at a certain point I need to do it. Remember, if you are at this hurdle you have already received the vision, timing, and inspiration now it's time to move. Remember, though research and conceptualization are important, you are not actually doing it until you are doing it. The question we have to address at this hurdle is, what's stopping us?

Stay in your lane

In Galatians 5:7-8, the writer is giving instructions to the readers. In doing so, he makes an observation and asks a very important question, "You were running a good race, who cut in on you?" This verse has always stood out for me. Have you ever been on the right track and moving in the right direction in your life only to have someone discourage you? Who cut in on you? Have you ever been content with the season of life you were in only to meet someone's new fiancé, walk into someone's beautiful new home, ride in someone's brand-new car or hear of someone's promotion on their job and begin to question your life? Who cut in on you? One of our hurdles to success is that of wrongly comparing ourselves to others. If I am not careful, this is something that will challenge me to this day. I have achieved the highest levels of education and made some impressive accomplishments throughout my life. But all it takes is for someone who is more successful, wealthier, and more highly decorated to cross my path and I can begin to question myself or be tempted to chase after things outside of my purpose in the hopes of elevating myself. There was a time I would write this off as simply being competitive. Then I learned that comparing myself to others was wrong in three ways. First, giving too much attention to someone else's life can cause a lack of appreciation for my own life. Focusing on what someone else has places our attention on what we do not have or what needs improvement in our lives. In and of itself, this is not bad until we forget about all of the good things we have and begin to devalue ourselves. Second, when we focus on what others have, we can develop a desire to elevate ourselves. Again, there is nothing innately wrong about wanting to be our best. But when the motive is because of what someone else has acquired or accomplished, then we are moving in the wrong direction. We also need to be careful of the desire to want to be elevated. What is our motive for wanting to be above someone else or better than someone else? Why do we have the need to feel important? This type of thinking can lead us down an insatiable path where we will never be good enough. This type of thinking, if unchecked, can also give us a God complex where we want power, praise, and control of all things. This is what the Bible refers to as vanity, which only leads to destruction and disappointment.

> **When we focus too much on ourselves, we forget about others. If fact, ironically, if we dwell too much on self-promotion we can actually lose ourselves.**

When we focus too much on ourselves, we forget about others. If fact, ironically, if we dwell too much on self-promotion we can actually lose ourselves. This leads to the third detriment of focusing on others. Focusing on others can distract us from our purpose. It is possible that we can currently be in the right place, at the right time, and doing the right things in life. Yet, if we spend too much time inspecting other's lives we can move away from our own path and begin to walk in someone else's. Since I was a teenager I have always enjoyed jobs where I was helping children and youth. This led me to a career in education, which I thoroughly enjoyed. However, I started to dabble in side businesses and found myself longing for the success of people in corporate America. I changed my career to working for a major corporation and was on a fast track to corporate leadership. God quickly interrupted that plan as I decided to leave that position to attend the seminary with the purpose of helping people again. What happened? I failed to stay in my lane. I could have easily been a wealthy, successful corporate leader, but that was not who I was, nor was that what I had been called to do. If not for the intervention of God, I would have lost myself in someone else's "lane." It is important that we stay in our lane in life. We can, and should, seek motivation from successful people, but not at the expense of ourselves. We also need to learn how to genuinely celebrate others' accomplishments and achievements without forsaking our own.

Don't give up

Have you ever watched a sporting event in which one team was losing by a large margin? After watching for too long we can sense their desire to make it stop. Why would anyone want to keep playing when they are losing so badly? In certain sports there is a term called the mercy rule. This is a rule that is in place to insure the dignity of a losing individual or team. When a team is losing by a large enough margin, the referee will approach the coaches of each team and seek an agreement to end the game more quickly. This is exemplary of what we experience in life at times. There are times when we start a venture with excitement and if too much time goes by without significant results we can feel as if we are losing. If you are anything like me, when you feel like you are losing you are tempted to give up. In boxing the term, "Throw in the towel," comes to mind. When a boxer is losing badly, in the effort to maintain his or her safety the trainer will throw a towel into the boxing ring, indicating to the referee to end the contest. Have you ever felt like throwing in the towel? Even for competitive people who will endure almost anything, there can be a temptation to give up on a job, or a relationship or even ourselves sometimes. Galatians 6:9 encourages us to not get tired of doing what is right because, at the right time, we will see results if we don't give up. When we give up on something, we might stop the process and miss the results. I have spent the majority of my life working in education. However, years ago I was offered the opportunity to work for a major corporation. I was actually hired under the pretense that a position would be created for me. Soon after my hire I learned that this actually was not going to happen. I found myself working in a position that I did not like at all with no hope of advancing into a position I desired. I was very tempted to quit and find another job. But instead, I decided to just keep working hard and find a way to enjoy what I was doing. It wasn't long until a person who was in a unique position in the company resigned and I was immediately offered his position. Once in that position I was afforded the flexibility to tailor the work to what I desired. In fact, I was even allowed to change my working title. This had never been done before. This turned out to be one of my most enjoyable positions of my career. In fact, the only reason I left that position was because I followed my calling into the ministry and relocated to attend seminary. Through that job I received financial bonuses for my work and was able to treat my family and friends to entertainment and sporting events in luxury suites as a benefit of my position. Neither my family, friends, nor I would have experienced these benefits if I would have quit. What things do we miss when we give up too soon? A deeper question to consider is why do we give up in the first place? Sometimes we give up when we become too frustrated and are simply tired of dealing with issues. Other times we give up when we are working hard at something and it seems as if we are wasting our time. Yet there are times when we give up because of feelings of defeat and insecurity. One of my former high school classmates went on to selection into the National Basketball Association Hall of Fame. In an interview prior to the ceremony he was asked if he ever imagined that he would be in the Hall of Fame as a professional basketball player. What he said was quite surprising. As a college standout he was drafted in the first round to a professional team. He said his rookie year was the worst basketball experience of his life. He said he felt like he didn't belong there, he wasn't good enough, and he should probably end his career. But he said he just kept working hard, eventually they hired a new coach, and he began to thrive. Can you imagine if he

One of the greatest hurdles to our success is the hurdle of giving up.

had retired after his rookie season? What about you? Are you in a situation in which you are questioning whether you are good enough, or if you belong and are contemplating giving up? Maybe you are good enough, but your circumstances just need to change. Maybe if you just keep working hard, other opportunities will present themselves to you and you will find yourself thriving. One of the greatest hurdles to our success is the hurdle of giving up. Navigate this hurdle by pressing forward, working hard, being consistent, and remembering what you learned in navigating the previous hurdles discussed above. You will succeed if you don't give up!

Become a coach

This very book is inspired by the words of a coach. Coaches, whether sports coaches or mentors in life, have an incredible impact on people, especially when they are young. I have been watching the summer Olympic Games for many years now, and have witnessed how once-prominent athletes have become coaches for today's generation of elite performers. As a leader in both educational administration and ministry, many of my leadership principles and much of my leadership style is modeled after effective coaches. I have met many people who have said that they aspire to become coaches, teachers, counselors, and mentors because of a significant connection to someone in one of those roles at a critical time in their lives. I am reminded of the apostle Paul's words to his mentee Timothy when he encouraged him to teach others all of the things he was taught. And this should ring true to us. There are two key aspects of this relationship between Paul, the mentor, and Timothy, the mentee. The first is what we have received. No matter who we are or how hard we have worked, our success was not achieved on our own. When I hear someone use the phrases, "Pull yourself up by your own bootstraps," or, "Put your big-boy (or big-girl) pants on," it begs two questions: Who gave us the boots? And who gave us the pants? We are all recipients of someone else's teaching, training, and wisdom.

Furthermore, we are the beneficiaries of those who have gone before us and opened doors for us. More directly however, those people in our lives who have trained, supported, and encouraged us throughout our journey are key contributors to who we are today. These are our coaches. When we take a moment to think of all of the coaches in our lives and all that they have taught us, this should bring an appreciation for us. God has, indeed, blessed us with people who have played significant roles in our lives. We should never forget nor forsake these people. The second aspect of Paul and Timothy's relationship is the imperative for the student to become a teacher. At a certain point, the mentee needs to become a mentor to others, teaching others what he or she has learned. Again, I was not a stellar athlete in college, but I learned significant lessons in athletics and life from my coaches and my experiences. As I grew older, I had the opportunity to serve as a coach, teaching others what I was trained. There is nothing more satisfying than seeing someone achieve success after applying what you have taught them. However, we remain humble when we realize that we are only teaching what we have been taught. Whether I have taught someone while coaching athletics or teaching an academic course in a classroom, the experience is the same. I experience the significance of my life's journey when I share it with others. This is how we remain inspired as we run with passion.

> **There is nothing more satisfying than seeing someone achieve success after applying what you have taught them.**

Do it again

Life is often compared to a marathon. It is a long race that requires endurance to reach the finish line. I agree with that notion. However, I would add that life is a marathon that consists of multiple races. Though we are on one journey, we have numerous experiences. Many of these experiences have a beginning and an end. I have had some childhood friendships in which we met, grew into close relationships, and were closely connected. However, due to time, separation from relocation, and life circumstances, our  friendships no longer exist. I have had jobs in which I was hired, trained, and enjoyed the experiences. Yet I have moved on from those jobs and into new ones. As stated in Ecclesiastes 3:1, there is a time and season for everything. As we navigate through life, wonderful relationships and jobs come and go, and great experiences are here today and memories tomorrow. It is important that we recognize those times and seasons. I will never forget the summer after my freshman year in college when I was running track. My teammate and I were driving running late to the meet due to a traffic jam. As I drove up to the stadium, I could see through the fence that my race was about to begin. We rushed to a parking space and I ran onto the track. The official was almost ready to start the race when I hurriedly checked in with him. The announcer was introducing our names as we were standing in our lanes. I had no time to warm up. In fact, I was rushing to take my jogging suit off and put my track spikes on as I sat on the ground in my lane. Having no time to stretch or warm up properly, the official commanded, "Runners take your marks." I bounced up and down a couple of times and took a couple of very brief stretches. I then ran the race and did pretty well. Imagine that … I ran and placed in a hurdle race where I had no time to warm up. Now I would never recommend that to anyone. But the point is, there was a time in my life when my body could sustain this. Today I am in good health at my age, but I would be foolish to try to jog around my neighborhood without properly warming up and stretching afterward. There is a time and season for everything. I was an average athlete to begin with. But there came a time I needed to change my focus from competing as an athlete to competing in life. The season of my life changed. I began to focus on graduating from college. After graduation from college, my season of life changed again. I gave my life to Christ and my season of life changed again. I could go on, but the point is that our seasons of life change constantly. Our job is to recognize those seasons. If we are attentive and strategic we can start and conclude each season with passion. It might be disappointing that we cannot perform in the same way as we did when we were younger. But we can transition into a new season with a new wisdom and perspective. You may find this hard to believe, but if you can embrace your new season with the lessons you learned from your previous season, where you are going will be better than where you came from. We have the ability to take our seasons by a storm (no pun intended). There might be some hurtful losses in a season or some victorious moments that we never want to leave, but in either case we can have a perspective of looking forward. I remember when I was a kid at an amusement park with friends. We would ride a thrilling ride, and as soon as the ride stopped we would run as fast as we could to get back in line as we shouted to each other, "Let's do it again!" What ever happened to that kid in all of us? Has life bogged us down so much that we have moved our focus away from our passion to dwell on our current circumstances? My encouragement to you is, "Do it again!" Maximize this season of life and recognize the transition into your next season. Embrace the change, apply what you have learned and do it again!

LIFE QUESTIONS

1. What distractions are keeping you from focusing on your purpose?

2. What experiences from your past are you finding difficult to forget?

3. Is there anything in your past that you have buried or locked away and don't want to address?

4. In what ways can God and others help you run with passion?

5. Who can you contact to partner with you in this process?

PRACTICAL STEPS

Because this chapter offered detailed steps for navigating your hurdles, this final practical steps section offers a brief summary of the strategies in this book, which I have entitled, Ten Hurdles to Your Success.

Step 1: The preparation

Before the race begins, make sure you know where you are going. Identify your gifts and pray for direction from God.

Step 2: The mindset

No one enters a race to lose. Don't start your race with a negative disposition. If you are operating with your gifts from God and God's purpose in mind, you will be victorious.

Step 3: The start

You can't win your race unless you actually start running. It is difficult to be successful in anything unless you try it. After you have planned, prayed about and strategized, do it! Don't be afraid to start. What are you waiting for?

Step 4: The focus

Remember to stay in your lane. The great thing about the race of life is that it's your life. You are not competing with others. God created you to be uniquely you. All you have to do is be the best you. Focus on your race, function in your gifts and achieve all that God has prepared for you.

Step 5: The approach

Don't be afraid of the hurdles in your life. Just as you were created with purpose, the same is true with hurdles. The purpose of hurdles is to be leaped over. In fact, some runners actually aggressively kick them down. Don't shy away from life challenges. With the strength of God, navigate over them or kick them down.

Step 6: The rhythm

Runners who run long distances are successful by reaching a stride that can be sustained. They know when to speed up and when to slow down their pace in order to align with their skill levels. As you navigate your life's journey, find your rhythm. Know when you need to speed up or slow down. Finding your rhythm will help you swiftly and efficiently run your race.

Step 7: The balance

Balance is critical to running hurdles. Because runners run full speed and leave the ground to leap over the hurdles, they must maintain balance. Likewise, there are numerous areas to balance when running the race of life. First you must balance enjoying life today with addressing pain and injuries from the past. Secondly, we must strike a healthy balance between working to achieve our goals and relaxing and enjoying the journey. Balance will help you to run with purpose, health, and joy.

Step 8: The passion

Sometimes life can really get us down and cause us to move with little energy or passion. We need to make up our minds that we will move from being passive to being people of passion. In your own context and in your own way, passionately pursue the life with which you have been blessed.

Step 9: The press

In this race of life, you might find yourself running well, running with a healthy stride, and making progress. However out of nowhere, circumstances and challenges may present themselves, causing you to become emotionally and physically fatigued. This is the time you need to press toward your goal and not give up. Sometimes the best results are achieved by the hardest press.

Step 10: The power

Through everything we do, it is important for us to know where our true power comes from. Self-will and discipline is a must, but they will only take us so far. Our strength and gifts will have impact, but can only last for so long. It is only by the power of God, through our Lord Jesus, and the power of the Holy Spirit that we can sustain the toils of life in our pursuit of victory. It is this power that enables us to run strong, get up when we fall, and experience true life after failure.

PERSONAL PRAYERS/REFLECTIONS

FAITH GOT UP!

One of my career experiences was working at a high school where, along with my primary responsibilities, I had the opportunity to coach both football and track and field. In track and field, I had the privilege of coaching both male and female athletes to run hurdles. As a hurdler, the one guarantee that you have is that, eventually you will hit a hurdle and fall. Thus, aside from the many hours of teaching strategies and techniques, the one concept that I stressed to all of the athletes was to immediately get up after a fall.

There is one instance that stands out from all of my coaching experiences in track and field. Though I was a part-time hurdle coach, I always made an effort to be with my runners at every track meet. However, there was a particular meet that I was unable to attend due to a scheduling conflict. Faith, one of my hurdlers, competed in that meet. The day after the meet, as I was walking through the campus, one of the runners hurried up to me and said, "Hey coach, did you hear about Faith?" I replied, "No, what happened?" The runner smiled and said, "I'll let her tell you herself!" Although I was curious, I have learned through my career the level of drama in which high school students tend to function. Therefore, I didn't take the excitement very seriously.

As time passed, another student hurried to me, gasping for breath, saying, "Hey Cantrell, did you hear about Faith?" I replied, "No, but you're the second person to come to me. What happened?" The student responded, "Man, it was cool, but I'll let her tell you herself!" I was growing curious to find out what happened, however my focus immediately turned to my job responsibilities, and that curiosity was placed on hold. Finally, Faith came running up to me with a smile on her face. "Coach, did you hear what happened?" she stated with excitement. "No, what happened?" I replied. "Coach, you should have been there! I was running the 300 hurdles and I was running really fast. As I got about halfway through the race, I fell!" At this point, she paused and looked at me as if she was non-verbally communicating how cool that was. With a confused look on my face, coupled with a half-smile, I responded, "Okay …." She then jumped back in to her story, "After I fell, I remembered how you always told me to get right up when I fall … so I did! I got up and finished the race!" But that wasn't the end of her story. She continued to say, "At the end of the race when I saw my time, I ran a personal record!"

It took a long time before I could tell this story without tears in my eyes. Though I wasn't there, I could imagine her sheer determination and passion to finish the race. I could imagine that her mindset was against allowing a fall to hinder her from reaching the finish line. I could imagine that she ran with more determination after she fell.

How about you? Do you navigate your life with determination and passion? Do you live everyday as if it were your last? Do you wake up every morning with a determination to cross the finish line by the end of the day?

No matter what failures you have experienced in the past, even if your past was literally yesterday, there is life after failure. In fact, the reality is that failure is not failure at all. Failure is actually an experience that serves as a key to our future success. Like with a bunch of unidentified keys on a key ring, we learn which keys don't work when they don't open a given door. But instead of immediately discarding the key ring, we move through each key until we find the one that fits the door we desire to open.

In our lives, we must passionately move with purpose to discover what works, and what doesn't as we pursue our calling and destiny. When we make a mistake, as dire as the mistake and as painful the consequences may be, we must make every effort to learn why we made the mistake and carefully strategize how to avoid that same mistake in the future. Furthermore, we must quickly move toward the next key to tap into our giftedness and our life purpose so that we can open the doors to our destiny.

A goal of mine is, clichéd as it may sound, is to live each day as if it were my last. In doing so, I find that I am living with purpose and preparing to answer the ultimate question, "What did you do with your life today?" God forbid that, when I look back over my life, I find that I have wasted my gifts, ignored my calling, aborted my purpose, and failed to make my best contribution to this world. I cannot imagine standing before God and hearing Him ask me, "Why didn't you get up after you fell? Do you realize how fast you were running? If you would have gotten up, you would have qualified!"

Are you living a life of mediocrity? Do you believe that you have a calling on your life, but for some reason you are afraid to pursue it? Do you feel like the failures of your past have disqualified you from achieving your God-given destiny? Or maybe you are successful in life by the society's standards. Maybe you have a great job, a great family, and things seem to be going well for you. However, deep inside, you feel like there is something more meaningful that you should be doing.

Whatever the case may be, I encourage you to live each day as if it were your last. Don't wait until it is too late to discover that there is something of great meaning that you have been designed to do. My heart's desire for all people is that when we come to the conclusion of our lives we can echo the words of the apostle Paul in Philippians 4:7, "I have fought the good fight, I have finished the race, I have kept the faith."

What this statement means is that he has fought with all his passion and intensity. So even when I sustained the greatest beatings in life, I kept fighting. It means, also, that I must finish what I have started. There are times when I could have fallen and stayed fallen, but I got up! Finally, through good and bad, I never forget that it is God who has created me, it is God who has gifted me, it is God who has carved out a space in this world where I can make a difference, it is God who sustains me, it is God who strengthens me when I am weak, and it is because of God that I have a hope that in the end, my living will not be in vain. So, I am saying, do what my student Faith did. Faith got up! And I love her name happened to be Faith. But let me parallel her name to our walk. It is by faith that we can get up when we fall. It is by faith that we believe there is life and life more abundantly in our future. It is by faith that we live, move, and persist. And it is by faith that our failures become the stepping stones to our destiny. So my encouragement to you is to get up! Fight the good fight, finish the race, keep the faith, get up quickly when you fall, and overcome the hurdles to your success.

TEN HURDLES TO SUCCESS

Hurdle 1 — *The preparation*

Hurdle 2 — *The mindset*

Hurdle 3 — *The start*

Hurdle 4 — *The focus*

Hurdle 5 — *The approach*

Hurdle 6 — *The rhythm*

Hurdle 7 — *The balance*

Hurdle 8 — *The passion*

Hurdle 9 — *The press*

Hurdle 10 — *The power*

ABOUT THE AUTHOR

Dr. Dwayne Cantrell is no stranger to failure. From failing classes throughout secondary school, to being academically disqualified from college he experienced academic failure. After quitting his high school varsity football team in his senior year and prematurely giving up on his college athletic career, he experienced failure in athletics. From financial failure through poor risk-taking and moral failure due to personal insecurities he failed his wife, his children, and his church. Through the power of Christ and with much humility he committed to counsel, guidance and hard work. Today, Dwayne is the founder and senior pastor of Living Victory Church in Bakersfield, CA and has earned two Master's Degrees and two Doctorate Degrees. He also serves as an administrator for a major university in Southern California. Most importantly his marriage was restored and he and his wife have been married for 23 years and they have two adult children. He is a living example that through faith, humility and hard work you can overcome the hurdles to success.

Author contact:
E. Dwayne Cantrell
dwayne@lifeafterfailure.org